Medieval SEAFARERS of India

Medieval Seafarers attempts to explore the dimensions of Indian seafaring from the sixteenth to the eighteenth centuries, a period of striking change and growth for the trade and traders of the Indian Ocean. The vitality and resilience of Indian seafaring, attested by both tradition and historical experience, is set against the growing colonial domination that changed the contours of the traditional maritime world. The interplay of colonial domination and indigenous enterprise found echoes in literature and popular traditions, examples of which are woven into the narrative tapestry of the book.

Born in Calcutta in 1955, Lakshmi Subramanian is currently Reader in the Department of History, Calcutta University. Her field of specialisation is Economic and Social History of Western India in the Eighteenth and Nineteenth Centuries, with special reference to business communities. She has a number of publications to her credit. Her recent monograph, *Indigenous Capital and Imperial Expansion in Bombay, Surat and the West Coast* (1996) was released by Oxford University Press. For the same publisher, she has co-edited a volume with Rudrangshu Mukherji, *Trade and Politics and the Indian Ocean World: Essays in Honour of Ashin Dasgupta*. She has edited and introduced a collection of essays by the late Dr Indrani Ray, *The French East India Company and the Trade of the Indian Ocean*. Her interests include classical Indian music and travel. She lives in Calcutta with her eleven year old daughter, Indu.

Other titles:

Boman Desai	*A Woman Madly in Love*
Frank Simoes	*Frank Unedited*
Frank Simoes	*Frank Simoes' Goa*
Harinder Baweja (ed.)	*Most Wanted: Profiles of Terror*
J.N. Dixit (ed.)	*External Affairs: Cross-Border Relations*
M.J. Akbar	*India: The Siege Within*
M.J. Akbar	*Kashmir: Behind the Vale*
M.J. Akbar	*Nehru: The Making of India*
M.J. Akbar	*Riot after Riot*
M.J. Akbar	*The Shade of Swords*
M.J. Akbar	*Byline*
Meghnad Desai	*Nehru's Hero Dilip Kumar: In the Life of India*
Namita Bhandare (ed.)	*India and the World: A Blueprint for Partnership and Growth*
Nayantara Sahgal (ed.)	*Before Freedom: Nehru's Letters to His Sister*
Rohan Gunaratna	*Inside Al Qaeda*
Eric S. Margolis	*War at the Top of the World*
Maj. Gen. Ian Cardozo	*Param Vir: Our Heroes in Battle*
Mushirul Hasan	*India Partitioned. 2 Vols*
Mushirul Hasan	*John Company to the Republic*
Mushirul Hasan	*Knowledge Power and Politics*
Prafulla Roy, trans. John W.Hood	*In the Shadow of the Sun*
Rachel Dwyer	*Yash Chopra: Fifty Years of Indian Cinema*
Ruskin Bond	*The Green Book*
Saad Bin Jung	*Wild Tales from the Wild*
Satish Jacob	*From Hotel Palestine Baghdad*
Veena Sharma	*Kailash Mansarovar: A Sacred Journey*

Forthcoming titles:

Chaman Nahal	*Silent Life: Memoirs of a Writer*
Dr Verghese Kurien	*Daring to Dream*
Duff Hart - Davis	*Honorary Tiger: The Life of Billy Arjan Singh*

Medieval SEAFARERS OF *India*

LAKSHMI SUBRAMANIAN

LOTUS COLLECTION
ROLI BOOKS

Lotus Collection

First paperback edition 2005

The Lotus Collection
An imprint of
Roli Books Pvt Ltd
M-75, G.K. II Market
New Delhi 110 048
Phones: ++91-11-2921 2271, 2921 2782, 2921 0886
Fax: ++91-11-2921 7185
Also at
Varanasi, Agra, Jaipur and the Netherlands

Cover depicts Daulat Khan attacking the British fleet.
Cover and photographs on pages 6, 8 and 38:
Courtesy: *National Museum,* New Delhi.
Photographs by Dheeraj Paul.

Typeset in Galliard by Roli Books Pvt Ltd and
printed at Gopsons Papers Limited, New Delhi.

Contents

*The Maratha Admiral
Kanhoji Angre.*

Acknowledgements

This book is a product of my long and lingering interest in India's maritime past—an interest that was awakened and sustained by the writings and researches of Dr. Ashin Dasgupta. Unfortunately, my own specific researches on Western India in the eighteenth century failed to capture the maritime dimensions of the region and got trapped within the compulsions of official European documentation which preferred to speak on Indian capital rather than on Indian seafaring, its triumphs and travails in the high seas during the period of Mughal expansion and decline. The account draws heavily on recently published works and is in the nature of a synthesised history rather than an original piece of research.

In writing this book, I have incurred a number of debts. I am grateful to the Department of History, Calcutta University, for making available its resources, to my colleagues and students on whom I have at times inflicted my views and doubts; Dr. Hari Vasudevan, Department of History, Calcutta University, who occasionally read my draft besides rescuing me periodically from the whims of the computer, and finally, I would like to place on record my deep appreciation of my daughter Indu's forbearance and patience in dealing with her mother's moods and silences in the last three months, when the manuscript was finally made ready. It is to her I dedicate this monograph.

Calcutta 1999 Lakshmi Subramanian

A Maratha battleship.

Seafarers and Seafaring

The Tradition

The tradition of seafaring was a well entrenched one in medieval Indian society. Bound by the ocean on three sides, the sub continent had developed its maritime profile even as the prevailing Brahmanical order imposed restrictions on sea travel and traffic. While the *Baudhayana Dharma Sutra* forbade orthodox Brahmins to engage in sea travel and traffic and prescribed severe penances and penalties for transgressions, its author Baudhayana was forced to admit that the Brahmins of the north were found frequently transgressing the scriptures. Manu, too, in his *Smriti* considered sea travel and traffic taboo for the Brahmins and declared that a Brahmin who had actually gone to sea was unworthy of entertainment at a *sraddha*.

> *Agardahi Garada Kundashee Soma Vikrayee*
> *Samudrayayee Vandee cha Tailika Koota Karaka.*
>
> (An incendiary, a prisoner, he who eats food given by the son of an adulteress, a seller of intoxicating liquor, he who undertakes voyages by sea, a bard, an oilman and a suborner to perjury were all offenders.)

The taboo on sea travel, did not, in all probability, extend to other groups in the *varna* order, particularly to those whose livelihood and professional interests derived traditionally from maritime enterprise. There were innumerable examples of Hindu maritime enterprise in southern India not to speak of the elaborate maritime orientation of Chola power in south India in the tenth and eleventh centuries. There were traders and merchants in medieval Bengal whose bards frequently sang of voyages to Simhala and beyond, and there were Gujarati merchants in the Indian ocean in the fifteenth century, all testifying to the continuing and enduring legacy of the seafaring tradition in medieval India among Hindus and Muslims alike.

Who were the Sindbads of the Indian seas is the first obvious question that comes to mind. Technically, as a group, seafarers and mariners are identifiable in every coastal society as one living off the sea in the most rudimentary manner—fishermen, boatmen, pearl divers and so on. These men—the subsistence people, if one could call them that—using the seas as their natural element were found everywhere in the Indian ocean. In the social hierarchy of India, both in ritual as well as in real terms, their status remained depressed. Thomas Bowery, the Englishman who left a detailed and graphic account of the countries around the Bay of Bengal (1669-79) noted that the Mukkuvars (literally divers) of the Coromandel were untouchables. It was obviously from coastal fishing groups and communities that early mariners were drawn. Initially, there was probably no occupational distinction between fishermen, seamen and traders; presumably, the coastal peoples performed a variety of functions before specialisation set in, and the first tentative steps towards long distance trading were taken. As the contours of maritime trade became more defined following the gradual integration of littoral economies, local coastal groups whose seafaring skills were considered indispensable were increasingly absorbed as sailors and seafarers and even allowed to participate in commercial traffic. Significantly, with the advent of Arab shipping and the extension of Indo-Islamic commercial contacts, the seafaring population of the littoral took to Islam and, over time, built up a seaworthy reputation for themselves. Seamen from Malabar, particularly of Calicut, enjoyed the reputation of being bold navigators and known for some reason, we are told by Abdur Razzak, as the 'sons of China'. Duarte Barbosa, the Portuguese chronicler, also commented on the nautical skills of Malabari boatmen who made use of small rowing vessels. Tome Pires, the Portuguese apothecary and the celebrated author of the *Suma Oriental* (1512-15), praised Gujarati seaman and observed that they did more navigation than any other people he had encountered. Some of them were great pilots with impressive navigational and nautical skills. Goa, too, produced seamen capable of physical strain and hard work. The clusters of Mukkuvar villages in the Travancore coast did not elude Pires' attention. He commented on their involvement in the region's maritime activity and noted that their business included, among other things, informing the people of the interior that argosies were coming in from the high seas.

Fishing and seafaring communities along the coast operated at more than one level of economic activity. Retaining their basic occupation and relying on their instinctive understanding of the sea, they also found themselves servicing a more complex range of economic functions deriving from trade and commerce. Pires' comment on the Mukkuvars is a case in point. With the development of long distance sea-borne trade, they found their nautical and navigational skills in demand, not to speak of the wide range of ancillary services every port required at the commencement and during the duration of the trading season. John Fryer, who spent as many as nine years travelling in India and Persia, described the boatmen who came for 'transporting the treasure to Fort St. George', a business that undoubtedly supplemented their income from their traditional occupations. They were robust men with 'long black hair tied up in a clout of Calicut lawn, girt about the middle with sash, in their ears rings of gold, those that were bareheaded were shorn of all to one lock which carelessly twisted up to be left for Perurnal'.

Piracy too belonged to the realm of seafaring and was like all other sea-related occupations, considered seasonal employment. This was partially related to the monsoon currents of Asia that determined sailing patterns and schedules in the age of sail on both littorals of the peninsula. Navigation could not be carried on at all seasons; this necessarily meant that all maritime occupations, including piracy remained seasonal. Barbosa commented on the fisherfolk of Porka (Malabar), 'their livelihood in winter season is naught but fishery, and in the summer, they live by robbery of all they find, and everything they can take on the sea'. Malabar in the sixteenth century was a major zone of piracy, a development that was linked to the temporary displacement of local maritime groups in the wake of the Portuguese offensive. On the eastern littoral, Portuguese adventurers and Magh raiders of deltaic Bengal were dreaded by both merchants and rulers.

The key players in the trading world of maritime India were of course the small time traders, the ubiquitous peddlers of Van Leurian vintage who bridged vast cultural and economic spaces within the ocean and thereby held it together. Traders themselves were of different categories, some seafarers in the strict sense of the term, others negotiating commercial enterprises from land. Given the caste restrictions on sea travel, Hindu merchant communities did not always sail. This did not in any sense undermine their links with the maritime world; on the one hand, their shore-based mercantile activities closely corresponded to the ebb and flow of oceanic trade. The distinction between seafaring traders and shippers and shore-based businessmen was apparent to early Portuguese chroniclers. Tome Pires found neither the Brahmins nor the Nayars of Málabar going to sea and concluded somewhat definitively that all the merchants of Malabar were Moors who had taken over the entire sea trade. Duarte Barbosa who completed his book in 1518 found 'great merchants, both Moors and heathen' in Cambay. Pires too, had no doubt that in Gujarat, the Hindus held the cream of the region's overseas trade and commanded such influence that they were able to employ men at arms to defend their ships. The actual business of sailing local crafts and ships was undertaken by low caste Hindus as well as Muslims; we find mention in Conti's account of sailors performing a rite to God Muthiah, a Hindu deity. On the south-eastern seaboard in the Coromandel, Hindu groups were active participants in the sea trade. The pride of place, however, in terms of numbers as well as of influence, was held by Muslim mercantile groups in all the sea lanes of the Indian ocean; the Gujarati Muslims rubbing shoulders with Navayats, Moplas and Chulias.

A decisive factor in the evolution of long distance maritime trade as distinct from early seafaring forays was the unravelling of the monsoon code and deploying it to facilitate long distance sailings. As Kenneth McPherson argues, 'It was this breakthrough that enabled sailors and merchants to shrug off the constraints of coastal trading and undertake regular long distance voyages across the high seas'. Indian merchants learned to harness the monsoons as early as the first century AD and along with the ancient Persians were largely responsible for the creation of the Indian Ocean world as a self-contained and sustained trading unit. There had been no such unity prior to the decoding of the monsoons, as people on the shore of the ocean used the seas sparingly and operated in discrete enclaves such as the Red Sea, Persian Gulf or among the islands of South East Asia. The discovery of the monsoon altered this scenario as larger spaces came to be incorporated into the realm of maritime activity.

The term monsoon, derived from the Arabic word 'mausim', was used by Arab geographers and travellers to describe the wind system of Asia comprising essentially the south-west and north-east air currents, *Mausim al Kawa* and *Rih al Saba* respectively. From April to September, an area of low pressure prevailed in the region from the equator to the Himalaya, and moist winds travelled in the direction of the vertical sun. These south-westerly trade winds enabled sailing from the East to the West. The north-east monsoon similarly enabled sailing from the East to the West. Traders very quickly realised the necessity of sailing with the wind. As the seventeenth century French traveller Jean Baptiste Tavernier commented, 'navigation in the Indian seas is not carried on at all seasons, as it is in our European seas, it being necessary to take the proper season, outside which no one ventures to put to sea. The months of November, December, January, February and March are the only months in a year in which you embark at Hormuz, with this difference, however, that you can rarely leave Surat later than the end of February. During the first four months a wind from the north-east prevails with which you may sail from Surat to Hormuz in fifteen or twenty days; afterwards veering by degrees to the north it serves equally well the vessels going to Surat and those coming from it, during this period the merchants generally reckon on spending thirty to thirty five days at sea, but if you desire to make the passage from Hormuz to Surat in fourteen to fifteen days you must embark in the month of March or at the beginning of April, because you then have the western wind astern all the way.' Once the monsoon actually hit the coast, sailing was virtually impossible and from June to August when the winds were at their strongest, the ports on the western and eastern coasts of India remained closed to shipping.

Sighting of appropriate landfalls was an equally important skill that had to be acquired by the medieval mariner. The precise location of sandbars and islands off the Malabar coast baffled Europeans as late as the eighteenth century. For Gujarat, the sightings of the Girnar mountains constituted an obvious clue. The approach to coastal Bengal was through a maze of estuarial seas and rivers which were so wide as to confuse even an experienced ship master. Consequently, masters with the requisite knowledge were employed. 'It is sensible,' wrote Ibn Majhid, the pilot of Vasco da Gama, 'that every man knows his coast best although God is all knowing, and it is certain that the Cholas live nearer to these coasts (Bay of Bengal) than anyone else, so we have used them and their *qiyas* as a guide.' Clearly, by the fifteenth century, a considerable degree of specialisation had developed in the business of maritime trade, the operation of which drew on a pool of resources and ideas.

The Setting

The Indian peninsula, situated at the vortex of the Indian Ocean, was uniquely positioned to bridge the Islamic world of West Asia with that of South East Asia, thereby holding the ocean together. Provided with a long, even if broken coastline, India accommodated a string of ports and commercial outlets on both littorals. Some regions were more prominent than others; maritime Gujarat in the sixteenth and seventeenth centuries overshadowed the Konkan, which in terms of geographical formation was a more typical maritime area. The Malabar coast with its unique relief and location was a core maritime region attracting a huge volume of trade and shipping. On the other side, there was deltaic Bengal which fostered considerable commercial activity. Further south, there were the long coastal stretches of Orissa, Andhra and the Coromandel, where trade was channelled through a cluster of small ports and outlets.

The Indian coastline, five thousand and seven hundred kilometers in length, is a geographical reality exhibiting contrasting features. Cape Comorin is the southern most point from which the Malabar and Coromandel coasts jut out and extend for a thousand miles, one north-westward and the other northward and then north-eastward. The surf of the Arabian Sea beats on the Malabar Coast and that of the Bay of Bengal on the Coromandel. Both the seas open broadly in a southward direction to the Indian Ocean. The Indian coasts are, for the most part, not indented by large inlets, the only significant ones being the Gulf of Cambay and the Rann of Kutch and the wider inlet of the Padma-Meghna rivers in Bangladesh.

The west coast of India was naturally endowed with numerous havens, creeks and roadsteads. The region at several intermediate points was able to draw from a rich and productive hinterland that yielded textiles, rice and pepper. The coastal stretch comprised five broad divisions—Sind and Makran, Kutch and Kathiawad, Gujarat, Konkan, and Kanara and Malabar. The Gujarat region along with that of Kutch was made up of minor and major gulfs, inlets and creeks. The two tongues of water known as the Gulfs of Kutch and Cambay entered the land mass to define the region of Kathiawad. The Gulf of Kutch itself was dotted by minor ports. The port of Gogha was a major outlet in the fifteenth and the sixteenth centuries, capable of receiving large ships of considerable tonnage—something that even the premier maritime city of Cambay in Gujarat could not entertain. The continual problem of silting in the upper reaches of the Gulf and the frequency of tidal waves meant that Cambay could not receive ocean going ships. And yet it was Cambay that was identified as the great city of the East stretching out her two arms to Aden and Malacca respectively. Diu and Surat emerged in the sixteenth century as important ports supplementing the commerce of Cambay. If these Gujarati ports lacked the advantages of a felicitous coast and natural harbourage, they made up for it by their access to a rich and productive hinterland. The deserts of Rajasthan and the saline wilds of Kutch meant that the ports on Gujarat's littoral became the principal outlets for north India's exports. A concourse of merchants from Cairo and Aden arrived at Cambay at the commencement of every trading season on the way to Malacca. There were Arabs and accompanying them were Abyssinians and Persians from Shiraz. The markets of Cambay housed an incredible variety of wares impressing contemporary travellers; Barbosa made an inventory of the Cambay goods in his meticulous manner; it was the great and wealthy kingdom of Gujarat and Cambay in 'which there are many horses, which they carry hence by way of merchandise to the kings of India, Arabia, Persia and many cotton muslins for veils and other white and coarse cloths of the same of which many ships take cargoes to Arabia, Persia, India, Malacca, Camatra, Melynde, Mogadoxo and Mombaca, also other coloured cloths of divers kinds, silk muslins, carnelians, gingelly oil, southernwood, spikenard, tutenag, borax, opium, fine indigo in cakes and other coarser kind as well as many other drugs unknown to us, but held in great esteem in Malacca and China and of great value such as cachopucho, incense in abundance from Xaer, abundance of wheat and millet, great store of rice, gingelly, grains, chick peas, haricot beans and many plants with pods, which do not grow in our country but here are good, cheap and carried everywhere.'

The Konkan stretch of the coast in its northern half was characterised by sandy spits intruding into muddy shallows close to the sea and by numerous creeks and navigable streams running close to the sea. Around Goa, the coast was more deltaic and broken by a number of estuaries. The coast supported a number of ports like Chaul, Dabhol, Goa, Vengurla—màking the Konkan an archetypal maritime region. These ports handled the lucrative horse trade that was of particular and enduring significance to the Deccan states. Horses from Arabia were brought to the Konkan ports from where they were transported to the hinterland. The Konkan ports handled a fair amount of coastal trade involving a range of export items like cotton cloths, rice, areca and betel. Of the ports, Dabhol held the pride of place until the early seventeenth century, when regular sailings were fitted out to Ormuz, Mocha and Acheh in North Sumatra. Further south, there were the Kanara ports of Mangalore, Onore, Kanara and Bhatkal all of which drew their export staples from the adjacent rice and pepper producing hinterland.

South of the Kanara littoral was the long stretch of the Malabar coast, five hundred and fifty kilometers long and which by virtue of its access to the vast pepper producing hinterland commanded a premier position in the Asian maritime network. The coast was relatively narrow in the north and south, wide in the middle section and was dotted with backwaters, creeks, lagoons and rich lush vegetation. Ibn Batuta (1325-54) found the region remarkably well-wooded. Describing a journey that he undertook, he observed that the land of Malabar extended from Goa to Quilon: 'The road over the whole distance runs beneath the shade of trees, and at every half mile there is a wooden shed with benches on which all travellers whether Muslims or infidels sit. At each shed, there is a drinking well and an infidel who is in charge of it.'

The direction of the monsoon winds in relation to the Malabar coast facilitated long distance sailings to and from its ports. Several of them became important in the course of the fourteenth and fifteenth centuries, notably Calicut, Cannanore and Cochin. Pepper was the region's staple export consumed throughout India and exported to West Asia whence there was a further shipment to the Levant. The Arabs were important carriers of pepper in the fourteenth and fifteenth centuries and enjoyed the goodwill of the rulers of Malabar, in particular the patronage of the Zamorin of Calicut. They settled down in large numbers along the coast, married into the local population to form a new community: the Mapillas.

A number of inhabited seaports was noted by the Portuguese when they entered the waters of the Indian Ocean for the first time in 1498. Tome Pires presented in his *Suma Orientale* an exhaustive list—Manjeshwaram, Mayporam, Kattakulam, Nileshwaram, Baliapatnam, Cannanore, Durmapatnam, Puthupatnam, Calicut, Tanore, Ponnani, Veleankode, Kranganur, Cochin and Quilon among others. Most of these ports were part of the region's coastal trading network leaving the bulk of the overseas trade to Calicut, the port par excellence frequented by Arab, Persian and Gujarati traders.

The eastern littoral, in contrast, commanded a much wider coastal plain, formed in parts of the great deltas of the Mahanadi, Godavari, Krishna and Kaveri. The coast was generally flat and sandy, interspersed with shallow rivers, some perennial, others not, and with sandbanks that blocked even large rivers. This meant that ocean-going ships over three hundred tons deadweight could not enter these rivers to take advantage of river transport or docks situated on the banks of these rivers. These natural obstacles meant that the region was not favoured with any one major entrepot port like that of Surat in Gujarat. Generally speaking, the northern part of the Coromandel because of its indented character with bays, headlands and promontories was regarded a safer region for ships to harbour in. Among the major ports, mention may be made of Ganjam, Bimilipatnam, Narsipore and Masulipatnam. The last in particular owed its prominence in the seventeenth century to its political links with the Qutubshahi kingdom of Golconda. The other ports were involved in brisk trading along the coast with Ceylon, Malabar and the Maldives. In the southern Coromandel, the ports of Karikal, Nagore and Nagapatnam handled traffic of some significance.

The maritime profile of the province of Bengal was not determined by its physical location and ecological aspect. Almost the entire province was deltaic, often described as 'new mud, old mud and marsh'. The coast was a maze of channels, swamp and mangrove jungles, the Sundarbans, making shipping hazardous and risky. Notwithstanding the difficulties of terrain, Bengal commanded an impressive volume of overseas traffic in the fifteenth century that was channelled through two ports, Satgaon on the Ganges and Chittagong at the mouth of the river Karnaphuli. Bengal exported considerable amounts of grain and textiles to South East Asia, Ceylon, Malabar and the Maldives; sailings to West Asia were not uncommon.

Workers of the Sea

Who were the maritime people inhabiting India's littoral and operating its commercial traffic? From which social groups and communities were they drawn? How were the regional trading systems held together and how were they accommodated within the larger political setup? How did trading techniques evolve? How did these seafarers perceive their political masters: could they expect political patronage and protection or were they left largely to their own devices groping for viable alternative strategies? These questions need to be answered in order to understand the evolution of coastal society, its vitality and dynamics. A coastal society has been described as a human, coastal frontier which is porous, flexible and unspecified. How far would this generalisation apply to Indian coastal society if one can treat it as an unitary whole?

One or two generalisations seem to be quite in order. For the most part, the business of sailing and trading, of taking the oars and sails and making the trip to conduct actual business as well as of large scale investment in the shipping business (owning ships, hiring out cargo space) appears to have been dominated by Muslim trading groups right from Gujarat to Malabar and beyond to Bengal in the high medieval period, between the fourteenth and sixteenth centuries. Hindu shipping in the Coromandel was the notable exception to this rule. Islamic commercial expansion had fostered conversions along the west coast in both Gujarat and Malabar as well as in the ports of Bengal and the Coromandel. Cambay was in fact a stronghold of Islam while Calicut accommodated major settlements of Muslim businessmen. By the thirteenth century, a sizeable Muslim community had coalesced in Gujarat, including not merely traders, shippers and seamen but also indigenously employed groups like oilmen, masons and people with miscellaneous occupations. By the fifteenth century, the Gujarati Muslim trader definitely emerged as the single most important agency for the carrying trade of the Indian Ocean rubbing shoulders with the Arabs in the western waters and with the Chinese and Japanese in the eastern. They were generally Bohras or Sunnis and took to the sea as traders and seamen. They manned their own ships, operated the freight business and export trade.

The multitude of traders, however, were non-shipowning merchants, small men peddling their wares and combining their annual trading ventures with the Haj. Identified as Patani Bohras in European documentation, they conducted small scale trading operations. They approached the freight merchants for cargo space and on payment of specified charges travelled with their cargoes that consisted chiefly of cotton textiles. Along with the Khojas, the Bohras, arguably the most visible commercial group in Gujarat, represented the two branches of the Ismaili Bohra community who faced persecution from the Turkish Sultans of Gujarat. It has been suggested that the overarching commercial profile of the Bohra community as an exclusively trading community stemmed partly from the legacy of discrimination and persecution.

Typically, a ship owning merchant was expected to make his money in one of the following ways. He could hire out his ship to several merchants by taking on a cargo of goods on commendation; the shipowner guaranteed to pay the shippers the value of the goods (principal) and an agreed-upon ratio of the profits unless the goods were unsold for any reason. The ship owner could also exercise the option of trading himself. Both Hindu merchants as well as Muslim peddlers made extensive use of the available cargo space let out by ship owners. The rates of freight were periodically determined in a meeting known as the Noorbundy in the eighteenth century in Surat. The small time trader or peddler was a persistent even if not an immortal figure in the trading world of the Indian Ocean and could not be edged out by big time operators. Abdul Ghafur, Surat's merchant prince, was unable to establish a monopoly control over the Red Sea trade in the seventeenth century because his calculations were undermined by the operations of the small traders whose intervention in the market seriously affected prices.

Hindu and Jain merchants collectively referred to as the Banias did not, as a rule, undertake voyages or even operate in any significant manner the business of shipping. Their operations were shore-based and fed directly into the overseas trading network. They handled the all important business of brokerage, retail trade, marine insurance and respondentia and banking. These functions became, over time, identified as Bania functions, although the term Bania itself had specific caste connotations. Drawn principally from the Veneeya (Bania) or mercantile caste, they constituted a cluster of both Hindu and Jain castes sharing professional interests and cultural traditions that were reinforced by an abiding adherence to a moral order. This order emphasised thrift, abstention, vegetarianism and non-violence. Their cultural preferences never failed to strike European travellers forcefully. Barbosa, for example, commented at length on their cultural preferences when he wrote, 'this people eats neither flesh nor fish nor anything subject to death; they say nothing nor are they willing even to see the slaughter of any animal; and thus they maintain their idolatry and hold it so firmly that it is a terrible thing. For often it is so that the Moors take to them live insects or small birds and make as though to kill them in their presence and the Baneans buy these and ransom them, paying much more than they are worth so that they may save their lives and let them go. When these Baneans meet with a swarm of ants on the road they shrink back and see for some way to pass without crushing them. And in their houses, they sup by daylight for neither by night nor by day will they light a lamp by reason little flies which perish in the flame thereof'.

Other high caste Hindu groups like the Khatris and Nagar Brahmins of Gujarat in particular could and did undertake Bania activities and thereby, enjoyed membership in professional trading guilds without being part of the formal Bania caste conglomerate. Bania merchants operated through a network of active and interdependent correspondents, whose links stretched into the interior making the flow of export staples from the primary production centre to the port in question possible. Brokers were of many kinds; there was a general broker based in the port city who guaranteed the supply of export commodities demanded by the merchant-cum-shipper, there were commodity brokers who handled the business of specific commodities. All brokers worked through sub-brokers or under contractors who maintained direct links with the artisans through a system of cash advances.

The sailors manning the ships were drawn from a variety of local coastal communities. In Gujarat, we hear of the Kharwas who were classified under Hindu and Muslim sub-divisions. The Muslim section of the community claimed Arab descent giving their original names as Nakhudas. Kharwas were also found plying boats in coastal and riverine traffic.

The exact number of crew in Indian ships is difficult to determine. The sixteenth century Persian travelogue *Anis ul Hajjaj* by Safi bin Wali Qazwini (1569-70) does not specify the number of crew. The Englishman Nicholas Dowton in 1612 pointed out that an Indian ship of one hundred and forty tons (clearly he was referring to the small variety) carried seventy five persons, of whom thirty two were the main members. Twenty of them were responsible for bailing water, eight were in charge of the helm, four in charge of the 'toppe and yards' and twenty young men for 'dressing several men's victuals'. The rest consisted of merchants and travelling pilgrims. We do not come across any references to the apparel of Indian sailors except that they often wore 'white with scull caps for their heads' as Fryer noted in the course of his travels in the seventeenth century.

Abul Fazl, Akbar's minister, was well informed about the average size of a crew in a ship and listed them accordingly in his manual, the *Ain*. The number of crew, he noted varied in accordance with the size of the vessel. In large ships, there were twelve classes. There was first of all, the Nakhuda or owner of the ship who fixed his course followed by the Muallim or captain who was expected to be familiar with the depth and shallow places of the ocean and with the star constellations to assist travelling by night. 'It is he,' observed Fazl, 'who guides the ship to her destination and prevents her from falling into danger.' The Tandil was an important member of the crew as he represented the common sailors, the Khalasis or Kharwas. The Nakhuda Khashab supplied the passengers with firewood and straw and assisted in shipping and unloading the cargo while the Sarhang or mate supervised the docking and landing of the ship and often deputised for the Muallim. In addition, there was the Bhandari who had charge of stores, the Karrani or writer who kept the ship's account and served water to the passengers, the Sukkangir or helmsman who steered the ship according to the orders of the Muallim. Some ships carried several helmsmen but the number never exceeded twenty. The remaining members of the technical crew were the Panjari who looked out from the top of the mast to sight landfalls or approaching storms, the Gumti who was responsible for taking care of the leaks and bailing out the water and Top Andaz or gunner who was required in naval encounters. The Kharwas performed the actual business of sailing; they set the sails and set free the anchor when required.

There was thus, a well-defined hierarchical structure that determined relations between various categories of the crew and their respective earnings. Abul Fazl noted that in the harbour of Satgaon, a Nakhuda received Rs. 44 as pay whereas in Cambay, he earned Rs. 800. The others earned considerably less, the Muallim received Rs. 200, the Tindal Rs. 120, the Karrani Rs. 50, the Nakhuda Khashab Rs. 30, the Sarhang Rs. 25, the Sukhangir, Panjari and Bhandari Rs. 15 each, the gunner or Degandez Rs. 12 while the Kharwa or common sailor enjoyed a better remuneration at

Rs. 50 along with food on a daily basis. In addition to monetary remuneration, the Nakhuda was entitled to four Karrani who were also given cabins.

The Navayat Muslims constituted a major trading community in the ports along the Konkan. They, too, were related to the early Arab settlers who had been cordially received by the ruling authorities of the Deccan. European observers commented on their skills and extensive trading concerns. They fitted out large ships and plied the lucrative horse trade which was vital to the military supplies of the Deccan kingdoms. The Navayats did not marry into other Muslim communities and maintained their separate identity. Later census reports identified five sub-divisions within the community which originally settled in Bhaktal but eventually spread to other parts in the Konkan. Goa, for instance, housed a large and affluent trading community of Hindu and Muslim descent. Hindu trading groups in the Konkan were not averse to the idea of sea travel; we have references to an influential community of resident Chatims in the Konkan and Kanara ports. In Bhaktal for instance, Hindu merchants were enthusiastic traders and as Tome Pires observed, 'The king who was always inland made a Chetti governor of the heathens in his kingdom as he has the most property and is a great merchant, and the governor of the Moorish people is Caizar, a Moorish eunuch who was a servant of Coajatar, the one of Ormuz.' Hindu traders were mostly Saraswat Brahmins, Pais, Kamaths and Shenoys, all of whom were engaged in retail traffic and brokerage. The Saraswats of Goa constituted the indigenous commercial elite and controlled the retail trade in spice. They were active in coastal trade and fitted out ships transporting rice and sugar. They migrated to Bombay in substantial numbers in the late seventeenth and eighteenth centuries and operated a number of joint commercial ventures with European traders. Goa had its share of Gujarati Banias as well. M.N. Pearson refers to a report dated 1646 which estimated that there were thirty thousand Banias primarily in Goa, Diu, Bassein and Daman. Seamen and sailors in Goa and other Konkan ports were predictably drawn from local coastal communities many of whom took to Christianity in the wake of the Portuguese advance. Early Portuguese chroniclers praised Goan seamen for their muscles of steel and capacity for hard work, but did not elaborate on their caste status.

The overseas trade of the Malabar was for the most part in the hands of the Mapillas who were referred to by Tome Pires as great merchants and good accountants. Their trading network was widespread and extensive; they traded as far as Cambay to the north and Pulicat to the east and to Ceylon and the Maldives islands further south. They not only controlled some of the principal ports along the coast like Cannanore, Calicut, Cranganore and Cochin but had access to important procurement centres inland. The Cannanore Mapillas exercised considerable political influence, so much so that Pires wrote of them, 'if the power of your highness (the King of Portugal) did not extend to this kingdom, it would already be in the hands of the Moors because a certain Mammale Mercar has become all powerful here.' Besides the Mapillas, there were merchants of varying nationalities, Persians, Arabs, Chinese not to speak of the Jews and Gujarati Banias. The Gujarati Banias had their own special quarters in Cannonore and maintained their agents and correspondents to facilitate the business of banking and brokerage.

The movement of goods through the waterways to the coast meant a natural interlocking of riverine operations with maritime traffic. The rivers, lagoons and coastal waters formed a complete and integrated transport circuit which was operated at various levels by an assortment of seafarers. A spice magnate was expected to own an assortment of rafts.

Pires was struck by the sheer variety and size of Malabari shipping. 'There must be,' he said, 'four hundred cargo boats in the kingdom of Malabar, some of these are large and some small, they are lades, ships with keels. They are made like this because the Malabar people usually sail along the province of Kalinga which includes the district from Comorin to Pulicat. As there is a channel between this land and Ceylon where the water in the middle is only one fathom and half deep at low tide and which is called the shoals of Chilam, they had to make lades. That is the reason why these people do not sail on the high seas except in fear and trembling.'

Boats, rafts and ships were operated by Tiyyas and Mukkuvars, traditional fishing and coastal communities who combined seafaring with other related occupations. Given their depressed status in the Hindu social hierarchy, they responded positively to conversions—Christianity and Islam. They constituted the crew of the vessels and were, in fact, the largest section of the maritime workforce. Their skill was universally recognised by export merchants who relied on them for the smooth operation of their mercantile network. They were among the few to know the art of transferring merchandise from rafts to ocean-going ships without allowing the surf to damage rice bales and pepper packages. They also acted as porters who handled loading and unloading operations and the business of plying boats while sifting pepper and cardamom. Ibn Batuta noted this in course of his travels and observed that, 'when any merchant has to buy or sell goods, they are carried upon the backs of men who are always ready to do so. Every one of these men has a long staff which is shod with iron at its extremity and the top has a hook. When, therefore, he is tired with his burden, he sets up his staff in the earth like a pillar and places the burden without the assistance of another. With one merchant, you will see one or two hundred of these carriers, the merchant himself walking.'

Batuta was even more impressed with the cosmopolitan character of the Malabar ports. Here, the foreign merchants enjoyed pride of place and could count upon a measure of protection and support. The head of the *pardesi* or foreign merchants, Batuta noted approvingly, was Ibrahim Shahbandar from Bahrein, an accomplished man of great attributes. His residence was the meeting place for other merchants who frequently dined with Ibrahim and discussed matters of business. Batuta also referred to Misqal, a ship master in Calicut, who was immensely wealthy and possessed a great many ships that traded in India, China, Yemen and Fars. 'When we arrived in this town,' Batuta observed, 'Ibrahim, the Shahbandar, the Qazi, Shaikh Shihabuddin and prominent merchants as well as the deputy (*naib*) of the heathen ruler named Qulaj came to meet us and they had drums, trumpets, horns and flags on their ships. We stayed in the harbour of Calicut where there were thirteen ships of China.' Quilon, too, was an impressive town, its merchants are referred to by Batuta as Suli (Chulias) possessing considerable wealth 'so much so that one of them buys a ship with everything in it and loads it with the goods in his stock.'

No account of Malabar's maritime world or for that matter of the Indian littoral is complete without reference to the Jala Dasyus or pirates whose activities were set out in great detail by Portuguese commentators and by officials of the European trading companies in the seventeenth century. Piracy was an old and common maritime occupation that predated the arrival of the Portuguese in Indian waters, but its definition and connotation underwent major alterations in the sixteenth century, when the Portuguese classified all traders who refused to adhere to their official system of monopoly control as pirates. This classification was reinforced by the actual displacement and dislocation local trading groups initially suffered in the wake of Portuguese aggression at sea. Defiance of the Portuguese system of control took the form of mounting attacks on Portuguese shipping and these increased in scale and incidence as the century progressed. The Malabari pirates were described by the Europeans as being mostly Muslims. Francois Martin in the seventeenth century found them by and large adhering to the Islamic faith 'mixed with a little Hinduism'.

The Coromandel, as pointed out earlier, was identified with a long stretch of coast and accommodated a miscellany of trading castes, both Hindu and Muslim. By the thirteenth and fourteenth centuries, Muslim merchants were identifiable as a powerful interest group. Ports in the southern Coromandel like Tuticorin, Kilkarai, Kayalpatnam and later Nagapatnam emerged as major centres of elite Sunni trading families who came to be known as Marakkaiyars or Chulias. The Marakkaiyars constituted an endogamous body of Tamil speaking merchants and ship owners who maintained close links with Arab centres of trade and pilgrimage, as well as with the major Muslim localities of South East Asia and the west coast of India. Edgar Thurston, celebrated ethnographer and author of the *Tribes and Castes of Southern India*, described them as a 'Tamil speaking Musalman tribe of mixed Hindu and Musalman origins, the people of which are normally traders.' He distinguished them from Labbais, another sub-caste of the Chulias who were also Sunnis but who were drawn from the lower strata of coastal society like fishers, pearl divers, petty artisans and weavers. Their social standing in relation to the Marakkaiyars was low. The author of the *Arcot District Gazetteer*, Mr. Francis, noted that the word Marakkaiyar was derived from the Arabic word *markab*, meaning boat. Tradition had it that when the first batch of immigrants landed on the Indian shore, they were asked who they were and where they came from.

In answer, they pointed to their boats which they described as being *markabs* and thereafter became known as Marakkaiyars. They did not intermarry with the other Muslims and confined matrimonial relations to their sub-caste. Community solidarity enabled them to build impressive fortunes in trade and enter the world of the Indian Ocean trade in a big way. Pearl diving was among their special interests with the Kayalpatnam Marakkaiyars emerging as leading merchants of pearls and chank across the Palk Straits. Susan Bayly refers to a copper-plate inscription of Kayalpatnam which mentions the leading members of the Marakkaiyar fraternity being endowed with honorific titles. The Labbais, in contrast, maintained a low profile and participated more visibly in internal trade, peddling and brokerage as did the Rawthers, another sub-caste of the Chulias.

What distinguished the Coromandel trading structure was extensive Hindu participation in overseas trade. Seafaring was an important part of the ancient Tamil tradition, finding expression in both literature as well as in political expansion overseas. Sangam poetry waxed eloquent about the trade and traders of Kaverippupatnam, the stamping of the Chola's famous tiger mark on the incoming goods and the benevolence of the Chola administration in matters of tariff duties. The *Pattupattu* referring to the city's merchants sang thus:

> *While bartering their trade goods, the traders of Kaverippupatnam*
> *Neither took too much, nor too little.* (Quoted in *History of Tamil Literature,* Sahitya Akademy, 1988.)

The extensive use and application of the indigenous term Taragan or broker was an indicator of the social acceptability of the mercantile occupation. S. Arasaratnam, in his work on the Coromandel, argues that in South India, there was a good deal of mobility across castes and regions and linguistic boundaries. The basis of mercantile organisation was territory, not a particular caste group. The mixed caste character remained an enduring feature of South Indian commerce. It was thus not entirely coincidental that in sixteenth century Malacca, merchants from South India were referred to collectively as kings and not by specific caste names.

The Hindu trading community was made up of Komaties, Beri and Balliga Chetties (Telegu) and Tamil Chetties. The latter were sub-divided into Vyapari Chetty, Kasukura Chetty and Nagarathar Chetty. The Telegu Chetties had a distinct edge over their counterparts in the business of shipping and overseas trade, but both groups continued to dominate the business of wholeselling and retailing, brokerage and banking.

The actual sailings were undertaken by coastal groups like Mukkuvans and Paravas. The latter constituted an important segment of the low ranking community of the littoral. They took to Christianity in the sixteenth century and thereafter steadily improved their social and economic status. Their occupational skills—fishing, diving and sailing—had always been in demand among the merchants and rulers alike, and they put these to good use in the course of the sixteenth century.

A recurrent theme in Bengali folklore is the sea voyages and exploits of the seafaring hero—a motif that reflects the strength of a collective memory of a well-entrenched tradition. The *Chandi Mangal Kanya* by Mukundram Kavikankan recalls and transmits the tradition of maritime enterprise and activity. There is for instance, a detailed account of Dhanapati Saudagar, the protagonist sailing towards Ceylon. The fleet that he commanded had seven vessels; the ship Mandakara led the way followed by

Duravara, Guarekhi. Sankhachuda, Simhamukha, Chandrapana and the Chotamukhi. Each of these had a specific function allotted. The Chandrapana, for instance, transported goods while the Chotamukhi transported provisions.

The poet elaborated on the perils faced by the hero at sea. The most hazardous of these seems to have been difficulties attending the proper sighting of landfalls and sailing for miles in the open sea. To quote:

> *Setubandhu Saudagar Paschat Karia/Chalilen Dhanapati Bahiya Bahiya/Alanghya Sagar She Dakhine Sthal/Pathike Jigyasa Koto Door He Sinhal/Lokomukhe Shuni Sadhu Simhal Kahini/Bah Bah Baoliya Daken Farmani/Ratri Din Chole Sadnu Tileka Na Rahe/Upaneet Saudagar Hoila Kalidahe.*
>
> Finding himself amidst the boundless sea, with no land to his right, the travellers asked, how far it was for Simhala's bright; and as he heard the tales of Simhala's glories from the locals, he tarried not but commanded the men to row on, and sailed on day and night with no moments wasted till he reached Sinhala, the promised land. (*Chandi Mangal Dhanapati Upakhyan*, compiled by Bijanbihari Bhattacharya, Calcutta University, 1966, pp. 230-231.)

The strength of the poetic imagination, while testifying to the obvious vitality of Bengal's maritime tradition, cannot, however, be reconciled with the actual historical reality that we encounter in the sixteenth century, when shipping and trade was dominated by Bengali Muslims and itinerant Gujarati traders. According to Tome Pires, the trade from Bengal in general, and Chittagong in particular, was in the hands of the 'Bengalas' who were merchants with great fortunes. A great part of the region's trade was conducted by Persians, Turks, Arabs, merchants from Chaul, Dabhol and Goa. In Barbosa's description too, the inhabitants of Gaur and Chittagong are seen to include numerous merchants of foreign origin including Arabs and Abyssinians. Persian shipping, it is mentioned by Sanjay Subrahmanyam, was particularly visible on the westerly routes from Bengal. This covered the routes to Cambay, the ports on the Konkan and Malabar coasts, the Maldives and the Red Sea.

The Tradition Revisited

It remains for us to evaluate some of the more common assumptions and generalisations that have informed historical studies of medieval trade and seafaring in India. Notwithstanding regional differences, the communal divide in occupations, Hindu domination of the shore and Muslim hegemony over the seas, held fast along the Indian littoral. Seamen for the most part were Muslim converts and it was on a Muslim sailing crew that a ship master relied. However, this did not preclude the growth and coalescence of a trading society on the littoral which maintained close links with the larger hinterland or the development of a common syncretistic tradition of ritual and faith that bound all members of the trading fraternity irrespective of caste or religion. This is not to suggest that there was an absence of dissensions within the coastal society. Caste rivalries tended to overlap into professional competition. This was suitably taken advantage of by Europeans—both the Portuguese and the Dutch built up client Christian communities among the coastal peoples to foster their own traffic. Coastal society was not a homogenised whole, moved by similar impulses and motivations. The divergence of interests among the mercantile population necessarily meant that their attitude to maritime affairs was not grounded in a common agenda.

The question however remains whether or not it is meaningful to speak of a common seafaring tradition or a distinct identity. At the level of nautical and navigational knowledge, Indian seafaring drew on a common tradition that enabled mariners to break the monsoon code and direct annual operations accordingly. The specific requirements of individual regions determined marine technology, the attributes of which are appreciated and accepted by all seafarers. Even more significant is the realm of the seafarers, experiences at sea, beliefs, fears, rituals, superstitions and expectations all of which served to generate a distinct ethos and autochthonous identity. Thus in Surat, both Hindus and Muslims assembled together at the mouth of the Tapi river and threw coconuts into the water as an offering. Another maritime superstition involved carrying a corpse or the bones of a dead man to a ship if it was apprehended that the ship in question would be overtaken by a gale. Linschoten wrote of the festivities that marked the departure in vivid detail:

'When that will make a voyage to the sea, they use at least fourteen days before they enter into their ships to make so great a noyse with sounding of trumpets and to make fiers that it may be heard both by night and day, the ship being about with flaggers wherever (they say) they feast their pagode, that they may have a good voyage.'

At the same time, rituals around actual or mythological figures emerged: we hear of an Islamic figure, Khwaja Khizr, referred to as the Mukallaf Il Bahr (Guardian of the Sea) and Khawwadur Bahr (One Who Traverses the Sea). Both figures were venerated as patron saints of sailors along the coasts, and in whose names a number of rituals were performed. The spatial spread of these rituals is what is worth noticing; these were observed as far as Sind in the west and Bengal and Bihar in the east. Similar rituals were not uncommon in the peninsula either. Thurston talked of Muslim saints venerated in the towns of Porto Novo (near Cuddalore). The most popular of these saints seems to have been Malumiyar who apparently in his lifetime was a notable sea captain. His fame as a sailor, Thurston wrote, 'has been magnified into the miraculous, and it is declared that he owned ten or dozen ships and used to appear in command of all of them simultaneously. He has known the reputation of being able to deliver from danger those who go down to the sea in ships and sailors setting out on a voyage or returning from one in safety usually put an offering in a little box kept at his darga and these sums are expended in keeping that building lighted and white washed.'

NOTES AND REFERENCES

The basic data for the description of the coasts, rivers, estuaries and ports comes from a number of reference works such as the *Imperial Gazetteer of India* (Oxford, 1907-09), District Gazetteers relating to the districts of the various provinces of British India. Of these, the *Gazetteers of the Coastal Districts of Ratnagiri and Kolaba* are particularly informative. Other works include *The Cambridge History of India* edited by E.J. Rapson (reprint, 1987), chapter 1 by Sir Halford J.Mackinder and O.H.K. Spate's *India and Pakistan* (Reprint, 1960).

Valuable secondary literature relating to the ports of India and to the monsoon systems include Ashin Dasgupta and M.N. Pearson, *Indian and the Indian Ocean 1500-1800* (Delhi, 1987), Kenneth McPherson, *The Indian Ocean, A History of People and the Sea* (Delhi, 1993) and S. Arasaratnam, *Maritime India in the Seventeenth Century* (Delhi, 1994).

Contemporary travel writings have been of immense importance in documenting the profiles of local merchant and seafaring communities. The travelogues that have been extensively used include Tome Pires, *The Suma Orientale* edited by A. Cortescao in two volumes (London, 1944), Duarte Barbosa, *The Book of Duarta Barbosa* edited by M.L. Dames in two volumes (London 1918-21), The *Voyage of John Huyghen Van Linschoten to the East Indies* in ten volumes edited by P.A. Tiele and A.C. Burnell (London, 1885), the *Selections from the Travels of Ibn Batuta 1325-54* (London, 1983 edition).

Monographs on maritime trade and shipping have been extensively consulted. Abrahim Udovitch's *Partnership and Profit in Medieval Islam* (Princeton, 1970) for instance, details the ramifications of the shipping and freight business engaged in by Muslim merchants. M.N. Pearson's

Coastal Western India (New Delhi, 1981) is particularly useful in identifying Hindu shipping interests.

For the Coromandel, extensive use has been made of Edgar Thurston's *Castes and Tribes in Southern India* (Reprint, Madras, Delhi, 1987). More recent works like Susan Bayly, ***Saints, Goddesses and Kings*** (Cambridge, 1989) and of V. Narayana Rao, David Schulman and Sanjay Subrahmanyam, *Symbols of Substance: Court and State in Nayaka Period: Tamil Nadu* (Delhi, 1992) and Sanjay Subrahmanyam, *The Political Economy of Commerce: Southern India 1500-1650* (Cambridge, 1990) have provided remarkable insight into the moral and material universe of coastal and seafaring groups like the Marakkaiyars.

The seafaring tradition in Bengal is well documented in both folklore as well as religious texts. The *Chandi Mangal Kavya* (Calcutta University, 1966) for example is replete with references to maritime trade and activity. The *Eastern Bengal Ballads* (University of Calcutta, 1932) compiled and edited by Dineschandra Sen also testifies to the vitality and strength of Bengal's maritime tradition.

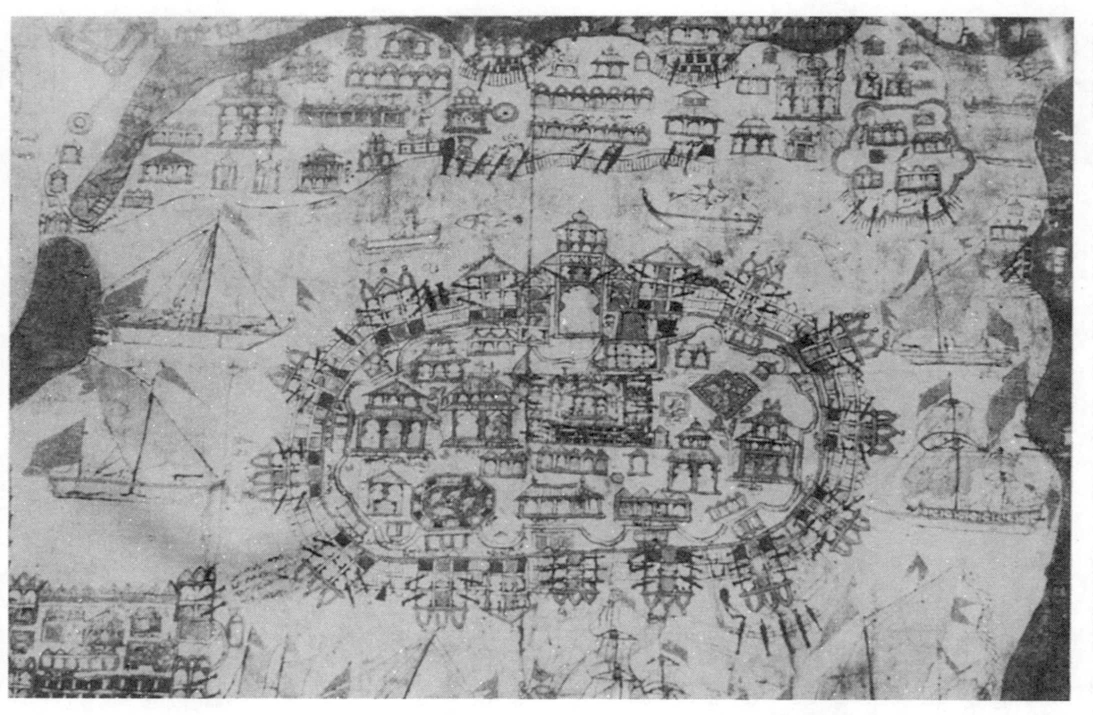

Map of Fort of Zanjira (off the coast of Maharashtra).

The State and the Seafarer

Wars by sea are merchants' affairs and of no concern to the prestige of Kings. Sultan Bahadur Shah of Gujarat (1528-37).

'And if the King's fleet (Aurangzeb) be but ordinary, considering so great a monarch and these advantages, it is because he minds it not, he contenting himself in the enjoyment of the continent and styles the Christian lions of the sea, saying that God has allotted that unstable element for their rule.' (John Fryer, *A New Account of East Indies and Persian Being Nine Years Travel 1672-1681.*)

These two assertions taken together, may well read as an indictment of the medieval Indian state's attitude of benign indifference to maritime matters. That there was no fundamental difference between the pre-Mughal authorities, the Lodis of Delhi and the regional sultans of Gujarat, Jaunpur, Bengal and the Deccan and the Mughal state in terms of their political conceptions or predilection is fairly clear. What is not clear is their inconsistent stand on trade and commercial affairs—in particular, the maritime space—which on the basis of existing evidence appears to have been ambiguous, ambivalent and often downright contradictory.

On the one hand, there was Nasihat Namas and Dastur al Amals that formally proclaimed the State's grand designs for economic development and laid down infrastructural foundations for the same such as the building of roads and rest houses and the establishment of mints for standardisation of currency. One has just to recall the twelve proclamations of Emperor Jahangir issued immediately after his succession wherein he promised that merchants travelling through the country would not have their wares exposed without prior consent. It was only when they were perfectly willing to dispose of any article of merchandise that purchasers would be permitted to deal with them without offering any species of molestation. It is undeniable that the age of Akbar and his successors saw the consolidation of an administrative and economic system which acted as a catalyst for commercial activity both on land and on sea. The administration of an admiralty in Surat and Dacca to oversee the operation of the Haj traffic as well as to combat piracy of the littoral and thereby support the commercial ventures of subject merchants is a case in point. Abul Fazl himself viewed the admiralty as an important auxiliary department expected to compliment the manoeuvers of the army besides safeguarding the 'benefit of the country in general', furnishing means of obtaining things of value, providing for agriculture and his Majesty's household. In his view, the sovereign had been guided by four principal considerations in building and extending the admiralty, none of which were specifically geared to the accretion of maritime power or even control of maritime trade. The objectives were by and large related to the consolidation of territorial power on land, to facilitate riverine expeditions and operations that involved 'fitting out of strong boats, capable of carrying elephants.... to be used in sieges and conquest of forts'.

The imperial fleet did not, therefore, stake well-articulated claims to maritime hegemony in the Indian Ocean. That remained very much a *mare liberum* accommodating parallel grids of control—local, coastal, European or Mughal. While the Mughal administration was more than willing to apply for European trading permits for their quasi-commercial ventures and pilgrimage tours, thus implicitly accepting European maritime control, they were certainly not impervious to the possibilities of driving a hard bargain with the foreigners on land which was the site for real and substantive contest. Early European observers were quick to detect the orientation of the ruling authorities. The Florentine merchant writing from Cochin in 1588 pointed to what he thought was an innate contradiction: 'with his courts and military camps, the great Mughal consumes everything even more than Vijaynagar did. His trade is as important as was that of Cambay, with the difference that it was not conducted by sea but by land.' The implications of such a clearly articulated preference for territorial control were hardly positive or beneficial for seafaring groups who did not have an official spokesman to back their claims against interlopers on sea. There were regional variations—Malabar was in more than one way an exception, as here, the sovereign and the ruling elite, while adhering to sea travel themselves, were motivated by considerations of revenue and power to keep sea channels open and trade and shipping free.

The Operation of Political Systems in India

A brief survey of the regional political systems in pre-Mughal India and thereafter, and their workings in the specific context of Portuguese empire building will enable us to identify the complexities and nuances of the dominant elite towards maritime trade and politics. A combination of tangible considerations was instrumental in engendering a specific attitude towards maritime matters which, it will be argued, did not directly enter the immediate revenue calculations of the regional and later the Mughal political systems. In Gujarat, the premier maritime region of India, political authority was for the most part of the fifteenth and sixteenth centuries, exercised by the Sultans of Gujarat. The two most enterprising of them, Mamud Begada (1450-1511) and Bahadur Shah (1526-37) busied themselves with what M.N. Pearson calls 'historical expansion' and consolidation of territorial power, co-opting important local and landed elements in the process. Direct control over the mainland was maintained by nobles and local elite groups whose support was enlisted by the ruling authority. The coast and the littoral were integrated into the larger political and administrative set up and controlled by nobles who combined office with interests in overseas commerce, a combination that modified existing conceptions of political authority and emphasised the maritime aspect of power of control. However, this did not result in the emergence of an autonomous coastal order capable of exercising independent political initiative in matters affecting local merchants and seafaring traders at crucial moments of confrontation and conflict.

The workings of the Gujarati political system came into sharp focus when the Portuguese challenge from the seas directly impinged upon the commercial priorities of the Gujarati merchant princes and their seafaring subjects. The initial thrust of the Portuguese was directed towards controlling the carrying trade in spices in the Indian Ocean. They used an injudicious combination of aggressive diplomacy and force to coerce merchants and rulers into submission. Attacks on shipping in the open seas directed from a series of strategic strongholds in the littoral kept up the pressure on local merchants who were expressly forbidden to traffic in spices. The second stage of Portuguese enterprise involved taxing Asian trade, the returns of which were expected to sustain the Portuguese seaborne empire. Both these objectives necessitated control of vital points along the littoral—Goa, Cochin, Diu and Malacca, all of which became the principal arteries of the Portuguese system of control. The organisation of the Portuguese seaborne empire, the logic of its expansion not to speak of its intent cut right across the interests of the state and the merchants in varying degrees. In Malabar for instance, the state's interests were thrown into serious jeopardy on account of its dependence on the pepper revenue. In Gujarat, the Portuguese claims did not fundamentally affect the power of the sultans or alter their political agenda in the mainland. The same, however, could not be said of the merchants of the region or even of the port officials, who had substantial investments in trade.

The two principal contenders of trade and political enterprise in pre-Mughal Gujarat were Malik Ayaz, Governor of Diu and Malik Gopi, Governor of Surat. Both of them were enthusiastic traders with extensive investments in the spice trade and were forced to negotiate with the Portuguese on their own. The negotiations were often undermined by the ambivalence of the Gujarati Sultans themselves as well as by personal rivalries and feuds both of which deflected the possibility of articulating a standardised position vis a vis the Portuguese and the larger issue of maritime power.

Diu in Kathiawad emerged under Malik Ayaz as a major trading centre. Contemporaries had occasion to comment on Ayaz's diligence in building up the port's commerce and in strengthening its defences. The establishment of a stable administration, the standardisation of fiscal payments and the enforcement of rules for the efficient handling of cargo and for safeguarding the safety of seamen combined to promote Diu's commercial profile. Tome Pires did not fail to note that at Diu, justice was better administered than in any other part of the kingdom. Ayaz's total income from the area under his control, according to Portuguese estimates amounted to nearly Rs. 3,20,000 per annum and half of this came from Diu alone. The returns from his personal trade were equally impressive; his ships were fitted out far and wide and his agents like Cherian Marakkar (posted in Malabar) were spread out all along the coast.

The range and ramifications of Ayaz's interests made an altercation with the Portuguese inevitable. In actual fact, however, his relations were not underscored by a clear cognisance of encroachment on his sovereignty or his sphere of influence. Malik, therefore, alternately deployed the collaboration strategy with that of confrontation and maintained very complex relations of solidarity and perfidy with the Portuguese. As Jean Aubin observes, 'he inspired among fidalgoes sentiments not the less diverse, maintained with some personal friendships and exercised a fascination to which even Albuquerque succumbed, divided as his various passages and letters show between esteem and animosity.'

Malik Gopi of Surat, Ayaz's rival, found in the Lusitanian challenge an excellent opportunity for self-aggrandisement. Commanding a personal fleet as well as excellent personal relations with the Sultan, his commercial interests were extensive enough to court the support of the Portuguese as a counterpoise to the influence of his competitor, Ayaz. This did not enhance his position substantively in the long run for he lacked territorial autonomy and was dependent for protection and patronage on the larger political edifice. If the interests of his overlord, the Sultan, happened to coincide with that of his governors, retaliation and confrontation against the Portuguese materialised. If it did not, a quick and ad hoc patch up of disputes followed.

The Sultans, by and large land lubbers, did on a couple of occasions react and respond to the challenge offered by the Portuguese. The challenge essentially involved a violation of the principles of free navigation and trade in the Indian sea that had so long been customarily enjoyed by the Indian seafarer, an encroachment on custom revenues of port towns like Diu and the installations of fortifications. For the Sultans, these demands were irritants to be sure but not substantive issues that impinged upon their sovereign authority. The centrality of these issues therefore remained questionable and whether the Sultan would contest these claims and engage in protracted hostilities for the reclamation of coastal forts and strongholds was tied to the larger political agenda of continental expansion. Portuguese attacks on trade and shipping continued right through the 1520s. These escalated into full scale hostilities in the next decade when a Portuguese armada actually entered the Gulf of Cambay. The Sultan retaliated but only for a while when he was relatively free from his more pressing concerns. In 1534, for instance, when he found himself fighting the Rajput states of Chittor and Mandu and the Mughal emperor Humayun, he lost no time in terminating hostilities and signing a peace treaty with the Portuguese. The 1534 treaty provided for the surrender of Bassein to the Portuguese. In addition, the Sultan accepted on behalf of his merchants the authority of the Portuguese *cartaz* as the only admissible trading permit which merchants had to avail of in order to operate in the trade of the ocean. The Sultan also agreed to limit Gujarat's naval expansion and not to use the forces it already had. The Portuguese consolidated their advantages further by holding on to Diu, where they were permitted to build a fort. This, as it turned out, proved to be a critical concession enabling the Portuguese to stabilise their operations in Diu, a vital point for the successful enforcement of the Cartaz-Cafila-Armada system. Diu was successfully defended on a number of occasions, in 1538 as well as in 1546.

The merchants of Gujarat could thus hardly count on the intervention of the state to deal with the problem of foreign aggression at sea even when it seemed to encroach on sovereign and territorial rights. The vulnerability of Gujarati shipping against Portuguese assaults was an important factor accounting for the relative readiness of Gujarati seamen to accept passes from the Portuguese captains and submit to their embargoes on the carriage of 'spices and Muslims'. However, this in itself was not tantamount to unilateral submission on the part of the seafaring merchants who devised ways and means of operating both within and without the official system of control. For the Sultans and even their successors, the Mughals, the Portuguese claims did not constitute a fundamental violation of sovereign authority or prerogative; glory, as M.N. Pearson points out, was not won at sea, it was firmly and visibly linked to land. 'The wholly military ethic of the Muslim rulers was bound up with land and the horses racing over the plains.' The notables, even those whose interests were linked to the coast and control of its resources, failed to articulate a policy of sustained resistance, largely because it did not materially affect their position, status or self-esteem.

In effect, therefore, the merchants were dealing with rulers who were largely impervious to maritime matters and with the politics of a new commercial entrant, the Portuguese, whose trading activities threatened to dismantle the carrying trade of spices in the Indian Ocean by building up a naval and maritime empire that would control and regulate all trading channels in the ocean. Further, in order to make the empire a self-sustaining proposition, the Portuguese adopted a policy of taxing the Asian trader through the Cartaz-Cafila-Armada system, wherein, merchants were left with one of two options: to defy the system outright or to function within its constraints. The merchants opted for the latter. Their decision to adapt to the new dispensation was a judicious one and paid off and resulted in the long run in a substantial expansion of Gujarati trade in the Indian Ocean.

In Malabar the situation took a different turn. The various principalities into which the region was divided derived their resources from trade and therefore could not afford to remain benign spectators to Portuguese action. Merchants were an important category whose interests had to be adequately defended. The position of the merchants was so well entrenched in the polity that their interests were guaranteed and buttressed by the state power. A new dimension was added to the merchant power in the course of the sixteenth century when traders like Mamale Mercar and Kunjali actively appropriated political power and carved out small quasi-autonomous fiefs. However, in the Malabar, politics was not exclusively oriented towards the sea. The ruler of Calicut, the Zamorin resisted the Portuguese in order to score off against the house of Cochin, a consideration that was as compelling as the one to protect his traders and the trade of his realm.

Malabar on the eve of the Portuguese arrival was divided into several independent principalities—the foremost of these being the ruling houses of Kolatiri or Cannanore, Calicut under the Zamorin, Cochin, Quilon and Travançore. Relations between these states were far from cordial, the Kolatiri Raja as well as the Raja of Cochin were antagonistic to the Zamorin who had by the fifteenth century emerged as the leading power on the coast. His authority was, however, periodically questioned by the Rajas of Travancore and Cochin while it was acquiesced to by other chiefs, like those of Cranganore and Idapalli. Calicut's politics was largely if not entirely determined by its central location in the pepper trade of the western Indian Ocean—a position which generated abundant revenues to the kingdom and an annual influx of immigrant merchants to the city of Calicut. The city in fact housed a substantial foreign population of Gujarati Muslims, Chetties and foreign Muslims. The Zamorin was bound to take special care of the pardesi who enjoyed an exalted status—on arrival, the foreign merchant had at his disposal a Nayar to serve as personal guard, a Chetty to look after his possessions and a broker to get goods for him. He had to pay them a fixed monthly salary which was supplemented by commissions paid to them by the supplier. In Cochin and Cannanore, the Mappillas were the dominant businessmen and were referred to as Marakkars, an honorific. In 1504, the Marakkars were divided into clans; Cherian Marakkar and his brothers and Mamali Marakkar and his brothers were both closely associated with the pepper trade. Cherian Marakkar, an agent of Malik Ayaz, was closely involved with the trade in Gujarat. In Cannanore, the Muslim merchant community was headed by a spokesman of the powerful Arakkal family referred to by the Portuguese as *Mamale de Mer* or Regent of the Seas. The entrenched presence of the merchant community in Malabar reflected the centrality of overseas trade for the Malabari kingdoms—in every sense, a lifeline for the perpetuation of which its rulers were prepared to shed blood. It was not entirely fortuitous that the encounter between Indians and the Portuguese should have been the most traumatic and violent in Malabar—an experience that not only endured in local memory but was recast later by nationalists in the twentieth century.

The Portuguese quest for Christians and spices brought them to the Malabar coast in 1498. At Calicut their arrival aroused only marginal interest. The Zamorin received them with due courtesy but would not entertain their claims. 'How could he', he asked, 'expel more than 4,000 foreign Muslim households who live in Calicut as natives, not strangers, and from whom his kingdom received so much profit?' Further, their demands for preferential treatment like exemption from custom dues were preposterous and could hardly be entertained. The Zamorin turned them down and in the process earned the undying hostility of the Portuguese who interpreted his action as part of a malevolent conspiracy. The second encounter under Cabral who succeeded Gama was even worse. A hot-headed and tactless officer, Cabral initiated hostilities against the Zamorin who took up the cudgels for independence and for the welfare of his merchant subjects. For the Portuguese, the conflict marked the first definitive expression of their maritime claims, their hegemony over the seas. Barros, their official chronicler, summed up their politics when he observed, 'It is true that there does exist a common right to all to navigate the seas and in Europe we acknowledge the rights which others hold against us, but this right does not extend beyond Europe and therefore the Portuguese as lords of the sea are justified in confiscating the goods of all those who navigate the seas without their permission.'

The Zamorin could hardly be expected to take kindly to these pretensions or to their intrigues that followed in the neighbouring state of Cochin. The Portuguese exploited the rivalry between Calicut and Cochin and made overtures to the Raja of Cochin. The Raja of Cannanore too, for a while responded to Portuguese initiatives, but the cordiality was short lived. Indiscriminate attacks on local shipping stiffened the attitudes of both the Zamorin as well as the Raja of Cannanore who entered into an agreement in 1505 to mount a major offensive against the Portuguese. The Zamorin built up his fleet and made substantial additions to it in order to restrict Portuguese operations at sea. Alberquerque noted this in his correspondence where he mentioned the Zamorin in possession of sixty *caturis*, all indigenously manufactured and positioned against the ships of Cochin. 'Calicut oppressed us with them because the factor of Cannanore did not dare to send coir or supplies in paqueres and parvis to Cochin for fear of being captured. The Calicut men watched them from mountain heights and any atalaya or parap they saw coming, they at once pounced upon them.' Clearly, the Zamorin's manoeuvres were able to intimidate Portugal's allies and restrict their aggression.

The Zamorin's intervention was viewed with increasing favour by the local merchants. Merchants based in Cochin found it viable to migrate to Calicut and take up residence there. In 1524, Ahmed Marakkar along with his brother

Kunjali Marakkar and his uncle Mohammad Marakkar took up permanent residence in Calicut. They received substantial patronage and protection from the sovereign who invested Mohmmad Marakkar with the title of Kunjali and with the office of admiralty. Kunjali exploited these concessions to build up his own base of operations and launch a systematic offensive against the Portuguese, intercepting their fleets and confiscating their cargoes. The strategy adopted was one of guerrilla warfare. Close encounters were as a rule avoided partly because of the inadequate range of firearms that Kunjali commanded. In due course, Kunjali himself began to entertain political schemes and appropriated the grandiloquent title of 'King of the Malabar Merchants and Lord of the Indian Seas' and made no attempt to disguise his intentions. They were not entirely compatible with his sovereign's sphere of control. In fact Kunjali's actions were definitely interpreted as encroachments on the Zamorin's authority—one popular story has it that Kunjali displayed his contempt for the sovereign by cutting off the ears of the royal elephant and castrating his Nayar sentinels.

Cannanore emerged as the second great centre of resistance where a merchant and state combined to operate against the Portuguese intruder and undermine the working of the Portuguese system of control. The resistance in the initial stages assumed the form of sporadic attacks on Portuguese settlements. These attacks expanded in scale and incidence even as Portuguese reprisals became more brutal. The capture of Goa by Alberquerque in 1510 strengthened the Portuguese line of defence and enabled them to step up controls over the pepper traffic in western waters. Merchants like Mammale were compelled to develop alternate channels of commerce and organise defence patrols along the littoral. The Mappilla merchants organised a coalition along the littoral and invested in patrol fleets that sprang up in Pokrad, Ponnani, Pantalayani, Kollam and Cannanore.

Paroas or row boats manned by twenty or thirty oarsmen were employed to oversee the clandestine pepper trade that originated in Calicut and ended in Cambay as well as to mount attacks on the Portuguese armada. The strategy paid off, the success enjoyed by Mammale and the Mappilla merchants was recognised and neither the Portuguese chief nor the Kolatiri chief were able to displace these ventures. Mammale for a while seemed to have succeeded in staking his claims to a miniature naval empire that dominated a section of the seas and commanded the revenues of a continuing sea traffic.

The exploits of Kunjali and Mammale were, however, exceptional instances of merchants assuming political initiative and staking concrete claims to maritime hegemony. The agency of control was the pass of cartaz which traders were obliged to accept, a gesture that privileged one authority over the other, in this case that of Kunjali/Mammale over the Portuguese Estado. For the local rulers like the Zamorin or the Kolatiri or the Sultans of Gujarat, the issue of naval or maritime authority per se was not central to their notions of control. The ideological implications of the pass were not as serious as the threat of blockade and embargo. The presence of the foreigner who did not subscribe to the rules of traditional commerce was an irritant in so far as it undermined the flow of revenues to the kingdom. It was not seen to encroach on the accepted realms of sovereignty. Even for the Zamorin, there was no question of sustaining indefinite hostilities at sea for the ideals of maritime power and hegemony.

The situation was fundamentally different in peninsular India. Here too, the attitude of the ruling elites to the larger issue of maritime jurisdiction and power was ambivalent and inconsistent. The empire of Vijaynagar which ruled over a substantial part of the peninsula in the sixteenth century was fully aware of the importance of free trade and therefore of the dangers implicit in the Portuguese stand. The South Indian sovereigns could not remain indifferent to the issue of the Portuguese monopoly largely because of the compulsions of the horse trade, the smooth operation of which was vital to the military agenda of Vijaynagar. Military reforms were closely linked to international commerce—a point that was amply attested by Deva Raya's attempts to establish deeper political control over the emporia trade of the west coast. Accounts of foreign observers confirm that the rulers of Vijaynagar offered importers high prices for quality horses, even dead ones so as to monopolise the trade in them. Vijaynagar's greatest sovereign, Krishna Deva Raya was perfectly cognisant of the overriding importance of commerce and acknowledged that a king was bound to 'improve the harbours of this country and so encourage its commerce that horses, elephants, precious gems, sandalwood, pearls and other articles are freely imported. He should arrange that foreign sailors who land in his country on account of storm, illness and exhaustion are looked after in a manner suitable to their nationalities. Make the merchants of distant foreign countries who import elephants and good horses be attached to yourself by providing them with daily audience, presents and allowing decent profits. Then those articles will never go to your enemies.' These canons of statecraft adhered to in theory, by Krishna Deva Raya and his successors did not, however, permit the formalisation of a maritime policy per se. Although, admittedly, the Portuguese did not enjoy the same position of strength in peninsular India, it is also undeniable that the State of Vijaynagar did not attempt to regulate the course of external trade in the same manner as they did the flow of revenues from land.

The disintegration of the empire was followed by the emergence and expansion of the Muslim sultanates of Bijapur and Golconda and the assumption of independence by tributary chiefs like those of Tanjore, Ikkeri and Senji. The fragmented nature of political control in peninsular India made it even more difficult to determine a set of attitudes to external commerce and to its regulation by the Portuguese. There were instances of confrontation between the Portuguese and the chieftains relating to allocation of custom payments and to the right interpretation of laws involving shipwrecks and the disposal of property confiscated thereof. Cesar Frederic in his account of Nagapatnam had occasion to mention points of legal dispute. 'The city is of a great genteel lord of the kingdom of Bezenagar, nevertheless, the Portuguese and all the other Christians there are well off, with churches and a monastery of St. Francis of great devotion, and well housed, but in the last analysis, they are in land of tyrants who at their will can do them any ill as occurred in the year 1565. If I recall it well that the Nale who is the Lord of the city asked for some Arab horses, and they having denied them, a few days later, this Lord came to see the sea so that the poor citizens this being an unusual thing had doubts that he came in dudgeon to sack their city and embarked with all the best things they had, the movables, merchandise, money and jewels and made to distance the ships from land but their luck was bad, so that the following night there was a great storm at sea, which flung all the ships against the shore, and all that could be recovered was robbed by the army which had come with the Lord and which was present on the sea shore.' The writer clearly disapproved of the Nayak's arbitrary claims to maritime property that found its way to shore during a storm as well as his attempts to intercept the horse trade as and when he pleased. The question, however, remained whether this act of confrontation constituted an integral part of an organic maritime policy.

Portuguese claims on the trade of the Coromandel were never very clearly spelt out or even implemented. Their settlements—Pulicat, Nagapatnam, Sao Tome de Meliapore—were unfortified notwithstanding the permission they enjoyed from the Nayak of Tanjore to erect fortifications. The absence of an effective base to send out flotillas to enforce the Portuguese cartaz and thereby control Asian trade meant that their share in the regions' trade was marginal. Acheh in North Sumatra became an alternate conduit of trading operations for Asian traders who undertook sailings through the Malacca Straits to Java and other ports in the archipelago.

Portuguese intervention was pronounced in the coastal trade between Coromandel and the west coast, the Cafilo do Coromandel. From about the middle of the sixteenth century, fleets of small coastal vessels owned in part by Asian traders were based on the Coromandel, and the rest were accompanied by a Portuguese escort fleet to provide the necessary protection against pirates and privateers. Clearly the local chiefs or Nayaks had not considered the necessity of organising security measures themselves as an alternative to Portuguese protection or even of defining the limits of their own maritime jurisdiction in the manner that the Angrias did later in the eighteenth century. As it happened, the Portuguese failed to accomplish their original design, that of monopolising the carriage of spices in the Indian Ocean and of regulating Indian trade in the manner that would service their far-flung empire. Trade remained free barring the occasional irritation caused by the enforcement of the cartaz; traders made their own options and on the whole, the experience of dislocation was confined to one or two commercial groups like the Arabs and the Muslims in Malabar.

Our impression of the trade of Bengal remains fragmentary. That Bengal maintained extensive links with the Indian Ocean is certain. Hussain Shah (1498-1520) is reputed to have maintained a powerful fleet. W.W. Hunter's statistical account of Bengal refers to the travels of one Shaikh Bhik of Gauda who was a cloth merchant and set sail for Russia with 'three ships laden with silk cloths and two of those ships were wrecked somewhere in the neighbourhood of the Persian Gulf.' Local traders also attest to Bengal's vibrant maritime tradition; mention is made of Arab merchants settled in Gauda for purposes of commerce and of Chamham Ali, a merchant from Bahgdad settled in Gauda for purposes of trade.

Hindu naval activity seems to have been organised around the centres of Sripura and Chandradvipa. Chieftains controlling these places owned and deployed commercial as well as military fleets. Pratapaditya, the ruler of Jessore for instance maintained a fleet of ships which were built and refurbished at Dudhali, Jahajghata and Chakaori. The Raja of Sripura resisted Mughal expansion and even managed to recover in 1602, the island of Sandvipa. The exploits of these Hindu chieftains were not exclusively maritime, like those of Kunjali; rather they were an admixture of territorial control on land with that over the estuary given the geographical contours of Bengal. At any rate, seafaring, shipping and overseas trading activity by the fifteenth century seem to have been considerably if not entirely Islamised. Indeed, the exploits of Hindu seafarers as eulogised in medieval folklore were representations of a cherished memory rather than of an objective reality.

The establishment of Portuguese power in deltaic Bengal was not accomplished by major political confrontations and collisions. In contrast to their operations in the west coast, the Portuguese activities in the Bay of Bengal were sporadic and in the nature of free-booting. Their skills as mariners and gunners were, however, widely acknowledged by the local rajas and later by the Mughal State. The Portuguese consolidated their settlements in Chittagong, Satgaon and later Hugli. Tensions between the Portuguese and the ruler of Arakan who controlled Chittagong until 1660 was a regular feature of coastal politics in Bengal.

The Mughals at Sea

The establishment and consolidation of the Mughal State introduced a new dimension to the world of Indian trading and seafaring. The Mughals like their predecessors were landlubbers. They were in their element on horseback on the plains. The sea was not their preferred site of action, that great unstable element which was not theirs to control or govern. And yet they could not choose to ignore it altogether; besides the advantages that accrued from the returns on overseas trade, there was the pressing business of organising the Haj in the seventeenth century. The organisation of the Haj to Mecca became a major compulsion enjoining the Mughal State to institute among other things the imperial admiralty in Surat.

The incorporation and integration of core maritime regions such as Gujarat and Bengal, the maintenance of transportation and communication channels that connected the imperial centre to far-flung areas of the subcontinent and the tangible presence of the state as a major consumer of agricultural and manufactured products underscored the power and hegemony of the Mughal State. This could not but have a catalysing effect on trade and commercial activity which was directly linked to the grid of revenue transactions, the bulk of which was commuted in cash. The Mughals insisted on revenue collections in cash thereby accelerating the pace of market transactions and monetisation. It was thus no accident that the seventeenth century constituted a golden period for Indian trade and shipping. The benefits of political security, the integration of the subcontinent into the larger Central Asian-Iranian-Turanian circuit, the expansion of West Asian markets under the patronage of the Ottoman and Safavid rulers were exploited by Indian merchants and mariners whose operations substantially expanded in scale and scope. Improved communications gave the merchants easy access to a large and productive hinterland whose goods entered the cargoes of sailing merchants. At the same time, the influx of bullion that came into India was central to the working of the Mughal economy and helped sustain the revenue and monetary edifice of the Empire.

Notwithstanding the obvious link between foreign exchange earnings and the economic well-being of the Empire, the ruling aristocracy's attitude towards maritime power or even control of foreign trade remained ambiguous. The Mughals did organise a naval department and admiralty but this was essentially intended to supervise the annual Haj to Mecca and to keep riverine traffic in the Indus and in the Tapi (off Surat) free from piratical incursions. The Mughal navy did not patrol the high seas nor engage in combat. On the contrary, it did not hesitate to solicit the assistance and intervention of the European powers to police the seas and curb the activities of pirates, privateers and the Portuguese. In fact, the North European trading companies were aware of their naval strength and used it whenever necessary to extract additional concessions from the ruling sovereign. These tactics did not, however, always pay off—the Mughals could and did get their own back by withholding permission to install factories in the hinterland. In fact as early as 1618, the Dutch somewhat ruefully informed their superiors that, 'it seems if we desire to trade in Surat and Mocha, we had best accord free passage everywhere to all Moors without distinction.'

The organisation of the annual Haj was a serious business for the Mughal authorities. After the conquest of Gujarat, Akbar appointed an officer entitled the Mir Hajji (Leader of the Pilgrims) to conduct a caravan from Hindustan to Mecca. The *Tabaqat i Akbari* of Nizamuddin Ahmed mentions that this was done most diligently, and that every year a party of enlightened men from Hind received provision for their journey from the royal treasury and went with the appointed leader to the holy places. 'Never before,' the writer mentions, 'had any monarch provided for the annual departure of a caravan from India nor had any one furnished the means to the needy to enable them to perform the pilgrimage.'

The tradition continued well into the seventeenth century as provincial viceroys sought to improve their personal credentials by taking a keen interest in the smooth operation of the Haj. Ghulam Hussain Salim in the *Riyazu-s-Salatin* commented on the energies of Murshid Quli Khan, the Viceroy of Bengal, in this direction as he used to, 'send every year copies of the Quran, transcribed by his hand, together with votive offerings and gifts through the headman of the pilgrims and other caravans bound for pilgrimage to Mecca, Medina, Najaf, Karball, Baghdad, Khorasan, Jidda, Basrah and other holy places like Ajmer, Panduah . . . . .'

The establishment of the Mughal fleet off Surat was not an original Mughal innovation. It was part of the Bijapur legacy that they inherited. The Bijapur rulers had entrusted the Sidis of Janjira, a powerful confederacy of coastal chiefs, with the responsibility of patrolling the seas to check minor instances of piracy. In 1636, Sultan Adil Shah of Bijapur agreed to pay tribute to the Mughals; Shah Jehan made over the Konkan to him and among the places ceded were Chaul, Panvel and Danda Rajpuri. To stabilise their control over the region, the Sultan of Bijapur entered into an agreement with the Sidis of Janjira, the latter assuming responsibility for protecting trade, combating piracy and transporting pilgrims safely to Mecca. The submission of the Sidis to Bijapur was not a smooth process; instances of rebellion and retaliation were frequent. Given the contested and fragmented nature of political authority in the Konkan, Bijapur as well as the Mughals had to deal with the pretensions of coastal chiefs of Maratha extraction not to speak of the encounters with Shivaji. It was during the Mughal-Maratha war in the Deccan that the Sidis transferred their allegiance to the Mughals and transferred their fleet to the service of Emperor Aurangzeb. The Emperor in return invested the leader of the Sidis with the office of the Imperial Admiral and an assignment of Rs. 30,000 on the revenues of Surat. The Confederacy at Janjira was also provided for: its various constituent chiefs were assigned important offices and a corresponding share of the revenue. In addition to the imperial fleet commanded by the Sidis, there was the Kachari fleet, a minor fleet comprising half a dozen small crafts intended primarily for watching the river and detecting the occasional smuggler. The imperial fleet was expected to safeguard coastal shipping and trade from the perils of piracy.

What did these elaborate arrangements amount to? The provision for the Haj and the construction of the fleet undoubtedly constituted important interventions and reflected a concern with security issues at sea. But how did these rélate to the larger question of maritime jurisdiction? The Mughals clearly could not be impervious to the benefits of international trade that brought in returns of silver and spices. Individual instances of caprice and oppression did not in any sense reflect on an anti-commercial ethos of the ruling administration. But it is equally obvious that the Mughals were not interested in contesting the European presence at sea, or even challenging the validity of the European trading cartaz that every seafarer including the Mughal prince had to apply for, or calling the European bluff when they threatened to blockade a particular port. Thus even if a seafaring merchant had the good fortune of enjoying the grace and benevolence of a particular governor, he could not expect official support as a matter of course on an issue that involved his interests. Further, the imperial flotilla did not assume specific responsibility for policing the seas but functioned essentially as an auxiliary force to assist the principal fighting forces on land. The patrolling of riverine traffic was the major concern of the fleets in both Dacca and Surat. Coastal and riverine trade in Dacca in particular was exposed to the raids of the Maghs and other local piratical groups. Contemporary reports are replete with references to Magh raids which were engineered from ships 'strongly made of timber with a hard core that canons could not pierce them'. The Mughal navy acknowledged the superior skill of the Maghs so much so that whenever hundred warships of Bengal sighted four ships of the enemy, if the distance separating them was great, the Bengal crew fled.

The improvements that were fitted out periodically on the imperial flotilla were largely in response to the requirements of security and conquest on land. The flotilla was put into extensive use during the Assam campaigns of Mir Jumla in 1662. The fleet that set sail on that occasion consisted of three hundred and twenty three ships. The same enthusiasm was not demonstrated by the Mughal State when it came to the question of protecting the trade of their own nationals on the high seas. In fact the gross inadequacy of the naval strength of the Mughal defence forces was revealed by their dependence on the European convoy services. On another occasion, they even solicited the Dutch for naval assistance in course of the Chittagong campaign in the 1660s, in lieu of which they promised to exempt the Company in perpetuity from the payment of custom duties throughout the empire.

Indian traders in the seventeenth century had thus to work out their own space in dealing with the Europeans. Indian seafarers operated from a position of relative weakness, deriving from the absence of state patronage and policy and falling back on the networks of personal connections and linkages with members of the ruling administration as well as with the officials of the European companies who had their private trading ventures to consider. The initial reverses that Indian merchants faced as a consequence of European activity in the Indian Ocean, when the English and the Dutch indiscriminately attacked Indian and Indo-Portuguese shipping did not prove irreversible. For one, the European superiority at sea was balanced by their weakness on land where they could ill afford to take on the Mughal forces. Europeans had to negotiate with the Mughal administration for permission to settle in the interior, to work out customs payments and so on. Further, the scale and orientation of European trading ventures did not fundamentally impinge upon the course of Asian trade in the Indian Ocean. The material change lay in the operation of the pass system which destroyed the freedom of navigation on the high seas that Asian merchants had enjoyed prior to the advent of the Portuguese. The benefits of the European convoy services were not lost on the Indian merchants who adapted themselves to the Anglo-Dutch system of passes and permits provided their traffic to West Asia was not severely compromised. The interests of the parties produced a broad consensus: the Mughals did not press for their advantage at sea knowing that their naval strength was inadequate; the Europeans realised that their growing investments in India lay at the mercy of the Mughals while the Indian seafaring merchant cut short his losses and worked within the confines of the European system of permits to expand his overseas ventures.

The Marathas and Politics of the Coast

The greatest adversary of Mughal rule in the seventeenth century, the Maratha leader Shivaji, exhibited a markedly different attitude to coastal politics and maritime power. In a sense, the specific configurations of the Konkan coast facilitated the articulation of a definitive maritime agenda for the Marathas in the seventeenth and early eighteenth centuries before the Hindu Pad Pad Shahi ideal tied them to an exclusively sub-continental project. The Konkan as a region guaranteed the essential conditions for sea power—ports, harbours, a hardy seafaring population and above all access to ship-building materials. The founder of Maratha power, Shivaji was not unaware of the significance and potential of sea power and made a resolute attempt to sweep the seas as he did on land. Admittedly, he found it more comfortable to negotiate on land but this did not blind him to the possibilities of sea power in concrete terms. The building of a string of coastal forts like Sindhudrug, Vijaydrug and Suvarnadrug, the organisation of a rudimentary navy and fitting out of annual naval campaigns against coastal potentates like the Sidis and the Portuguese spoke of an abiding and concerted engagement with the notion of naval power and maritime hegemony. Historical information on Shivaji's maritime activities is, however, neither accurate nor substantial. Contemporaries like Krishnaji Anant Sabhasad suggested that Shivaji's fleet was four hundred vessels strong. The Portuguese observer Cosme e Guarda pointed out that the fleet barely consisted of twenty-five ships, all of which were purchased second hand. On record, the Maratha navy consisted of five kinds of fighting ships. Of these, the most important were Ghurubs and Gallivats followed by Shybars and Manjhuas all of which were used in combat. The ships were under the charge of Muslim Nakhudas while the bulk of the common sailing and fighting crew consisted of Kolis and Bhandaris—fishing castes of the region known for their hardy constitution and endurance. They are said to have manned the fleets of the Sidis and later of the Bombay Marine, the naval arm of the English East India Company.

Shivaji's naval expeditions seem to have been directed principally against the Sidis of Janjira, a confederacy of powerful coastal chiefs along the entire stretch of the Konkan.

The Sidi claims were frequently contested by other aspirants like the Portuguese and coastal potentates like the Angria in the latter decades of the seventeenth century. Janjira was never conquered by the Marathas but the struggle continued unabated, occasionally involving the English East India Company authorities of Bombay. The wintering facilities that the English Company provided for the Sidis were viewed with disfavour by Shivaji. The English often found themselves in a tight corner. They were in no position to dismiss the Sidi's requests nor could they ignore Maratha pressure. The matter was resolved in 1679-80 after a dramatic engagement which secured for the Marathas the occupation of Kenery island adjacent to Bombay. The gain was subsequently ratified by a treaty concluded between Shivaji and the English East India Company. But the occupation of Kenery did not materially enhance the maritime profile or power of the Marathas. The Sidi's fleet remained unbeaten, their island base at Janjira remained secure and freedom of navigation remained an elusive and unrealised ideal.

The endeavour was, however, not entirely fruitless. It served as a legacy for Shivaji's successors, notably the Angrias, to expand and consolidate. The Angrias were a coastal family in Kolaba, and whose interests Shivaji had for a while promoted. It was left to them to put forward definitive claims of maritime supremacy and take up arms in defence of their rights. The coastal offensive under Kanhoji Angria in the first decades of the eighteenth century was impressive and for a brief while it seemed that the Angrias would, with the battle of the seas, control navigation and defy the vested rights of the Europeans. In the claims and counterclaims of the Angrias and their rivals, Indian and European, the sovereignty of the seas was fiercely contested, and for a brief while it seemed that indigenous maritime power would dislodge the importunate pretensions of the European trading companies.

Conclusion

The rise and fall of the political regimes in medieval India did not fundamentally alter the entrenched political attitudes to the idea of maritime hegemony and control. Political authority in India either at the all India level or at the local level preferred to stake its strength on the basis of territorial control rather than on mercantile control involving taxation on trade and protection of client merchants on the high seas against political competitors. The compulsions behind the choice are not easy to identify particularly in view of the flourishing state of India's overseas trade in the sixteenth and seventeenth centuries and of the Mughal state's consumption of bullion supplies. Clearly, the notion of power and sovereignty was inextricably tied to land and warfare on land. This engendered a particular warrior ethic that was not oriented towards the sea. Maritime jurisdiction did not figure in the developing political agenda of the Indian sovereigns. Rather than take on the Europeans in the high seas in pursuit of principles of free navigation, the Mughals like their predecessors preferred to work out a compromise formula whereby the Europeans were permitted, indeed, even authorised to police the sea and decide on the terms of navigation for the Indian merchants. The choice was not entirely free of immediate advantages. Indian seafarers and merchants showed themselves adept at manoeuvring within the new system of European controls and building up a substantial enterprise for themselves. In the long run, however, their inherent vulnerability vis a vis the Europeans surfaced particularly in the aftermath of Mughal decline, when Indian trade was stripped of its institutional basis. This in turn emboldened the peripheral powers, the European companies, to fish successfully in the troubled politics of the hinterland.

Notes and References

Recent researchers on maritime India have contributed to a better understanding of the linkages between the littoral and the hinterland and of the relationship between rulers and merchants in pre-colonial India. Of these, the works of M.N. Pearson, Ashin Dasgupta, Sinappah Arasaratnam, Om Prakash and Sanjay Subrahmanyam have proved particularly illuminating. See for instance, M.N.Pearson, *Merchants and Rulers in Gujarat: The Response to the Portuguese in the Sixteenth Century* (Berkeley and New Delhi, 1987) and *Coastal Western India: Studies from Portuguese Records* (New Delhi, 1981) and Ashin Dasgupta and M.N. Pearson (eds.) *India and the Indian Ocean 1500-1800* (Delhi, 1987). The workings of the Portuguese system, the relationship between the Portuguese viceroys and the sultans and governors of Gujarat are brought out in vivid detail in Pearson's *Merchants and Rulers.* Jean Aubin's essay 'Alberquerque et les Negotiations de Cambaye' in *Mare Luso Indicum* (1971) highlights the multiple levels of the Gujarati political system, the workings of which precluded the articulation of an uniform and cohesive maritime policy on the part of the governors like Malik Ayaz and Malik Gopi.

Standard studies on the Mughal empire do not emphasise its commercial agenda or lack of it for that matter. The benefits of Pax Mughalica and the expansion of Indian overseas trade in the context of Mughal expansion and consolidation, the integration of the Indian Ocean trading grid in response to the rise of the three empires, the Mughal, Safavid and Ottoman, have been elaborated by Ashin Dasgupta in his *Indian Merchants and the Decline of Surat 1700-1750* (Weisbaden, 1979) and *Merchants of Maritime India* (Variorum, 1994).

For the regulations of Emperor Jehangir quoted in the chapter, see *Memoirs of the Emperor Jehangir Written by Himself and translated from a Persian Manuscript* by Major David Price (Calcutta, 1904). The constitution of the Mughal admiralty, its composition in terms of personnel and functions is discussed in the *Ain i Akbari* by Abul Fazl Allami and translated from the original Persian by Blochmann. (Reprint, Calcutta 1977). The encounter between the Mughals and the Maghs of Arakan forms the subject of Jamini Mohan Ghosh's study *Magh Raiders in Bengal* (Calcutta, 1960).

For an understanding of the political system in South India in the fifteenth century and thereafter, see Burton Stein, *Vijaynagar* (Indian edition, 1994) and Sanjay Subrahmanyam, *The Political Economy of Commerce: Southern India 1500-1650.* (Cambridge, 1990).

Maratha maritime and naval activities are discussed at some length in Dr. S.N. Sen's classic work *Military System of the Marathas* (New Delhi, 1958) and Sir J.N. Sarkar's *Shivaji and His Times.* (Reprint, New Delhi, 1973). See also James Douglas, *Bombay and Western India* in two volumes (Reprint, 1985) for an archetypal English assessment of Shivaji's maritime profile.

A number of works have been published on the activities of Maratha coastal chiefs in the eighteenth century, notably Kanhoji Angria of Kolaba, the Sidis of Janjira and the Desais of Savantwadi. See for example John Biddulph, *The Pirates of Malabar* (London, 1907), S.N. Sen, *Readership Lectures to the Calcutta University* (Calcutta, 1931). More recently, we have Aniruddha Ray (ed.) *Minorities on India's West Coast: History and Society* (Delhi, 1991).

Indian Seafarers and the Europeans 1500-1800

European documentation is replete with references to Indian seafaring groups, their activities, their traditions and techniques, their trading pursuits and practices. These references have, over time, tended to inform much of our impressions on the nature and orientation of Indian maritime activity (not to be equated exclusively with trade) and its operators, the seafarers. It is only of late, that serious historical research has attempted to correct many of these received impressions and reconstruct the world of the Indian seafarer as he fought, sailed, prayed and plied the seas in search of his livelihood. Scholars have, however, recognised the potential of existing historical documentation which still remains the basis of our enquiries on the Indian seafarer and his interaction with the Europeans.

Indian Merchants and the Portuguese Encounter

The advent of the Europeans into the world of the Indian Ocean was even to the seasoned seafarer something of a shock. Even before Vasco da Gama had left the roadsteads of Calicut in a huff (three months after he had landed) threatening the most dire of retributions, the resident merchants of Malabar had a fair inkling of what they might expect over the next few years. The contempt and ignorance that Gama displayed of the rules of the game and the etiquette of trade sent ripples among the Asian trading fraternity as they braced themselves for the next round of confrontation. The articulation of Portuguese claims which involved enforcement of monopoly control over the carrying trade of spices in the Indian Ocean and the methods adopted to realise them were hardly compatible with the interests of the free trader and the networks which he operated in the Indian Ocean. The great seas he had plied for so long in complete freedom were no longer free—a fact that had serious implications. Indeed, the Portuguese style of trade and warfare, their claims over the right to mastery of the seas, constituted a violation of the agreed conventions and came as an unprecedented challenge for the Indian seafarer and merchant.

That the Portuguese meant business was evident by the speed and ease with which they organised their seaborne empire in Asia to realise their project of maritime hegemony. The discovery of the Cape route gave the Portuguese access to Asian spices and thereby opened up immense possibilities of trade and profit. From the very outset, therefore, they were resolved to dominate the carrying trade in spices in the Indian Ocean, which in turn would cut into the prospects of Arabs and Gujaratis in the Indian waters and the Italians across the Levant. The establishment of monopoly trade required the occupation of vital coastal strongholds from which the Portuguese could direct attacks on Asian shipping. Thus sustained attacks on local shipping in the high seas was accompanied by the occupation of coastal stations that became centres of policing and patrolling commercial activity in the sea-lanes. The authority of the Portuguese empire, which was but an aggregation of coastal forts, was articulated through the agency of the cartaz or trading permit, the acceptance of which was made mandatory for every trader and seafarer. Hereafter, every seafaring merchant had to equip himself with the Portuguese pass, pay customs at Portuguese stations and abide by new conventions that restricted the carriage of spices and pepper to Portuguese owned vessels. At the same time, the enforcement of the pass guaranteed the periodic payment of custom duties at select Portuguese stations and generated the necessary revenues for the maintenance of their seaborne empire. This necessity eventually overweighed considerations of an absolute monopoly of the carrying trade in spices which was even otherwise impossible to enforce. Regulation of Asian trade became the watchword of the Portuguese in India. Under the circumstances, an element of coercion became central to the structure of relations that developed between the local seafarer/trader and the Portuguese and moulded very significantly the coastal society's perceptions of the European factor at sea. One significant variant of the seafarer's response to the European intervention was resistance which the Portuguese preferred to treat as unlawful activity or piracy—a construction that was subsequently reinforced by the North European trading companies in the seventeenth century. However, the interaction between seafaring society on the coast and the Portuguese was not restricted to the domain of commerce and exchange. The Portuguese in Asia combined other activities with those of trading, notably missionary activity which enabled them to enter local society and in some cases alter its existing configurations. Thus the Portuguese encounter enabled communities like the Paravas of Tamil Nadu to regroup themselves and improve their relative position vis-a-vis other peer groups. It also helped iron out differences from a position of advantage that adoption of a new religion, Christianity, gave them.

Researches conducted over the past three decades have indubitably demonstrated the failure of the Portuguese to dismantle the trading networks in the Indian Ocean. Their activities reinforced the existing patterns of commercial exchanges and even enlarged their scope by the discovery of new markets. The failure derived from the discrepancy between policy and practice, a gap that was amply taken advantage of by enterprising trading groups to retain and even expand their commercial ventures. The sustained expansion of Indian commercial shipping in the late sixteenth and seventeenth centuries notwithstanding, Lusitanian pressure is well documented and exposes the inherent fragility of the system of controls that the Portuguese system instituted. But to argue that the advent of the Portuguese and their politics was of no consequence whatsoever to Indian maritime society would be far-fetched. The temporary displacement of local commercial and seafaring groups, who were denied access under the official system, the conquest of port towns such as Malacca, Cochin and Diu, resulted in a redrawing of maritime frontiers and commercial networks. Militarisation of coastal society notably in Malabar, the introduction of armed trading in the high seas, the acceptance of Portuguese as the lingua franca in maritime Asia and the wide currency of the cartaz as the new agency of maritime control among indigenous coastal chiefs and potentates in the seventeenth and eighteenth centuries along the littoral represented multiple facets of the Portuguese impact on the trading world of the Indian seafarer. The following section proposes to identify and delineate the multilayered dimension of the Portuguese presence in maritime India and how this moulded coastal society and experience in India.

The Organisation of the Portuguese Seaborne Empire

The formal organisation of Portuguese power in India evolved in distinct and identifiable stages. Unable to effect satisfactory bargains with ruling potentates over the expulsion of Arab commercial groups, their chief rivals in the carrying trade of spices in the Indian Ocean, the Portuguese took recourse to aggression at sea. Merchant shipping was indiscriminately bombarded. Sporadic assaults became more systematised in due course as the Portuguese successfully occupied coastal strongholds thanks to the insular attitude of the ruling potentates who were easily persuaded to part with them. The selection of the coastal strongholds was not entirely random; there was an obvious logic behind the choice of coastal points that strung together to become the Portuguese seaborne empire. In 1503, the first fort was built at Cochin, in 1505 and 1507, Sofala and Mozambique became tributaries respectively. In 1509, a combined Gujarati-Egyptian-Calicut fleet was defeated off Diu by Francisco D'Almelda. Important conquests in land were effected during Albuquerque's governorship from 1509 to 1515. Goa was taken in 1510, Malacca in 1511 and a fort built in Ormuz in 1515. Access to these widely dispersed points enabled the Portuguese for a while to spread the dragnet on Asian shipping. Portuguese fleets scoured the seas attacking Muslim shipping on sight. The display of maritime power and naval superiority was spectacular and as M.N. Pearson observes, Albuquerque dreamed not unseriously of disposing off his Muslim enemies by diverting the Nile to the Red Sea or alternately by raiding Mecca and holding the Prophet's body to ransom.

The orientation of Portuguese policy was at the outset, targetted at the Muslim trading networks (Gujarati/Arab/Mappilla) that dominated the sea-lanes of the Indian Ocean. If the first encounter under Gama's overbearing manner had been just inexplicable and annoying, the second encounter was downright provocative. Instructions for the voyage were explicit and laid down that all Muslim ships were to be attacked on sight and that the Zamorin, the ruler of Calicut, was to be persuaded to expel his foreign Muslim residents from the city. Armed with these directives, Gama peremptorily demanded cooperation from the Zamorin in the expulsion of all Muslims from the trade of the Indian Ocean. The Zamorin, not unexpectedly, refused to accede to this preposterous set of demands. How could he, he asked of his Portuguese adversary, 'expel more than 4000 households of them who live in Calicut as natives not strangers and from whom his kingdom has received so much profit?'

The early casualties of the Portuguese attack were equally indignant. They resolved to resist as they found their ships indiscriminately attacked by the Portuguese fleet. It was only after these attacks became seemingly unstoppable and damaging, that seafarers and traders were forced to forsake valour for discretion and opt for a more viable solution. They decided to take stock of what was an unfamiliar situation to say the least, and respond to its requirements. Response naturally was not homogenous as it varied from one group to another, given the plurality of merchant identities, and even from region to region. In fact it was only in Malabar that anti-Portuguese opposition was most sustained and articulate.

The initial bewilderment of Gujarati merchants at the new and arbitrary claims of the Portuguese and their aggressive tactics gave way to anger and retaliation in self-defence. Sometimes, Gujarati Muslim traders simply attacked to make their protest and defiance felt. Their attacks were from time to time encouraged by local coastal authorities whose interests had been seriously jeopardised by the Portuguese claims. Malik Ayaz, Governor of Diu, for instance, was an influential ship owner and merchant and found his commercial ventures seriously threatened by the Portuguese presence. Gujarati merchant retaliation was, however, on the whole shortlived. Neither the merchants nor the rulers were able to bring effective pressure or naval intervention to bear upon the Portuguese. The only option for the ruler was to accommodate those Portuguese claims at sea and on the littoral which did not directly impinge on their larger territorial interests and sovereignty. The strategy of the merchants was to adapt to the new system of control and exploit its gaps to their own advantage. Further, there was a shift in the priorities of the Portuguese agenda; the compulsions of private Portuguese trade and the compulsions of empire resulted in a relaxation of the initial system of controls, permitting merchants and seafarers to operate and even extend their maritime ventures.

Serious gaps undermined the effective functioning of the Portuguese system of controls. The net for one, did not cover important points like Aden which in effect meant that channels of communication for Asian shipping in the Red Sea remained open. Year after year, the Portuguese fleet witnessed instances of evasion on a large scale. In 1562, the armada saw fifty ships slip past and venture out into the Red Sea. A second weakness, as M.N. Pearson points out, was the marginality of Portuguese presence on the mainland and their subsequent dependence on local rulers and potentates. This did not always yield the desired results. Very often, the local authorities intervened to interrupt supplies of export staples, at other times they would arbitrarily raise the rates of custom duties payable by the Portuguese, rendering them at par with local traders. A third loophole in the system was the failure to establish custom houses at strategic points thereby making it easier for local traders to evade payment of custom duties so vital to the maintenance of the Portuguese seaborne empire. To this was added, the growing importance of private Portuguese trade in Asia which necessarily accommodated Asian commercial enterprise and cooperation and undermined the efficacy of official controls. As M.N. Pearson observes, 'it was more important that people trade and pay duties, than that enemies be denied trade with ships owned or licensed by the Portuguese.' What all this meant, therefore, was that the temporary derangement caused to Asian trade and shipping by the capture of Malacca and the introduction of armed force in the ocean which was offset by the rise of alternate centres and the regrouping of commercial and maritime networks in the Indian Ocean. The reassembling of local merchant enterprise cut effectively into the Portuguese efforts at monopolising the spice trade between India and Europe. More significantly, the Portuguese had no control whatsoever in the distribution of spices within Asia. Thus, largely because of the gaps in the Portuguese system of controls and the compulsions of private Portuguese trade, the empire in terms of a rigid set of control mechanisms ceased to be a monstrous monolith with its tentacles spread far and wide, choking off all channels of traffic.

At a more immediate level, however, the authority of the empire was real enough to the seafaring trader and his scheme of things. The acceptance of the cartaz testified to the major change that the Portuguese seaborne empire had effected in the realm of maritime power. For the first time, the sovereignty of the seas was being openly appropriated by the Portuguese, who through their official spokesman, Joao de Barros, argued that by common law, the sea was open to all but this applied only in Europe to Christians who were governed essentially by the principles of Roman law. 'For even though there does exist a common law which allows all navigators to sail the seas freely, this law applies only to the whole of Europe and its Christian inhabitants, who have been placed within the fold of the Church of Rome by baptism and by faith, and who are also governed by Roman law in their polity. But as regards Muslims and Heathens, who are outside the law of Jesus Christ, which is the true law that everyone has to keep under pain of damnation to eternal fire—if these are condemned in their souls, being the principal part of them, their bodies which are animated by those souls cannot plead the privilege of our laws, since the adherents of those creeds are not members of the evangelical congregation, even though they may be our neighbours as rational beings and though they may live to be converted to the true faith.'

Hindus and Muslims thus had no claims to right of passage in Asian waters after these had passed on to the sovereign authority of the Portuguese. They were thus empowered by the recent victories to claim sovereignty of the seas and to confiscate the goods of all those who navigated the seas without their formal permission. From this developed the Cartaz-Cafila-Armada system, the operation of which was expected to bolster the newly formed seaborne empire. Seafarers and traders were obliged to apply for the cartaz and avail of the convoy services of the Portuguese cafila and armada. The cartaz gave the trader the official consent to navigate, the convoy and armada assured him protection in the high seas against piracy and, in return for those services, the trader paid custom duties at select Portuguese custom houses as specified in the cartaz.

The practice of applying for and securing cartazes became so pervasive that it continued well into the eighteenth century when the Portuguese position was considerably undermined by the success of the North European trading companies. The relationship between the merchants and the Portuguese captains mediated through the agency of the cartaz stabilised over time, marking the end of open defiance from the Gujarati seafarer. The merchants' compliance was viewed with disapproval and contempt by both Gujarati and Portuguese chroniclers. It was deplorable and yet inevitable—only what could be expected from the Gujaratis, especially the non-Muslim groups who were weak and effeminate. Joao de Castro was contemptuous of the Gujaratis who he claimed were hardly men, and that all women of all other nations were more formidable than them in dexterity, strength and courage as well as in the practice of warfare and battles. The seafaring merchant had in all probability his own story to tell, one which underscored his anxiety and vulnerability before the armed tactics of the Portuguese and the continental preoccupation of his sovereigns.

Merchant Response in Malabar

Merchant action in Malabar, by contrast, followed a markedly different trajectory. It may be recalled that the Portuguese action was particularly violent and destructive in Malabar for it was here that opposition to the 'foreigners' (i.e. Portuguese) and their claims was direct and long drawn. The very first words that accompanied the Portuguese landing in Calicut were hardly encouraging:

> *'What the devil has brought you here?'*
> *'We have come in search of Christians and spices.'*
> (Portuguese reply to Tunisian Muslims upon landing in Calicut, 21 May, 1498).

The self-righteousness of the Portuguese and their inept and brazen dealings with both merchants and rulers in Malabar made confrontation inevitable. Misconception and misunderstanding was marked on both sides. Gama was ignorant of commercial etiquette and conventions, a deficiency that stood in the way of effective communication and negotiation. He was therefore easily convinced even in his first encounter that the Muslim merchants were intractably hostile and were actually plotting the ruin of Portugal. This fear soon became a paranoia and set the agenda for his successors. The bombarding of Calicut by Cabral and the establishment of contacts with Calicut's rivals like Cochin, Cannanore and Quilon sharpened the opposition and drew the lines of demarcation more clearly. Cochin became the nodal point for enforcing the system of controls and coercion. All flotilla was permanently stationed to oversee shipping in the Arabian Sea and organise attacks on all those who dared defy the Portuguese cartaz.

The anti-Portuguese opposition was taken up by the Zamorin of Calicut who emerged as the chief spokesman of the Muslim merchants in Calicut. He extended his fullest support to the merchants and launched a series of attacks on Cochin. A permanent state of hostilities between Calicut and Cochin prevailed in the following decades. Muslim shipping continued to function defying Portuguese controls whenever possible and accepting them whenever necessary. In many cases, there was outright resistance under the patronage and leadership of coastal chiefs like the Kunjalis or Mammale of Cannanore who emerged as merchant rebels staking claims to maritime hegemony. The militarisation of the seas that followed encouraged displaced groups to take to aggression on the high seas—a development that Portuguese writers preferred to describe as 'rebellion' or 'piracy'. This categorisation was subsequently reinforced by official and non-official European discourse in the seventeenth century. Francois Pyrard had no doubts in his mind when he wrote in 1607 of the Malabar pirates who had, 'an understanding with the Samory . . . they give him money and pay him tribute underhand. I am aware of this from having accompanied the captain, Cousty Hamede, when he went to treat secretly with the king's officers which he did only by night for fear of being seen.'

The seafaring community in Malabar, on their part had no doubts about the culpability of the Portuguese. The *Kerala Brahma* or Chronicles of Kerala described the atrocities on the seas thus: 'The Portuguese were responsible for the unmentionable atrocities on the sea. The Feringi ships alone did not keep the peace. The Mahomedan ships were the special objects of their fury. Every ship had to carry safe conduct issued by the Portuguese captain. But even with that, they were not safe. The Portuguese seamen demanded heavy bribes and baksheesh, and if whatever they asked for was not given the ships were confiscated.' The *Tuhfat al Mujahadin*, on the other hand, perceived the Portuguese intrusion as a calamity that was ordained by Allah. 'The Muslims of Malabar lived a happy and prosperous life on account of the benevolence of their rulers, their regard to the time honoured customs and their kindness. But the Muslims undervalued the blessings of the Allah and transgressed. So Allah set on them the people of Purtkal who were Christians. The Portuguese scoffed at the Muslims and held them up to scorn. They prevented the Muslims from their journeys especially their pilgrimage to Makka. They plundered their properties, burnt their feet and burnt them away. They put to death hajjis and other Muslims with all kinds of cruelties and reviled publicly the Apostle of Allah.'

The advent and aggression of the Portuguese in local perception, Muslim and Hindu, was co-terminous with calamity—a perception that moulded the making of coastal society in Malabar. Society became militarised as an endemic state of warfare was produced and perpetuated by Portuguese policies. The arming of the Mappilla population was one obvious external manifestation of this new and disturbing tendency. It dated from Cabral and Gama's offensive and escalated as Muslims countered the Portuguese blockade by developing a system of guerrilla warfare to resist their attacks and assaults. Shallow draft vessels were employed in these attacks. Francois Pyrard noted with consternation in 1607 that the Muslim residents of Calicut were all armed and that all their time was taken up with 'soldiering and they all knew the use of arms'.

Pyrard like all other chroniclers did not find a legitimate distinction between local trade and piracy. All trade that was conducted outside the official Portuguese system of controls was clandestine and contraband. To him, pirates were simply those who defied Portuguese controls and even attacked their shipping. Among them, the Malabaris were the worst offenders who considered piracy as good a profession as trade. What Pyrard was actually referring to was the sustained counter-offensive that indigenous shipping in Malabar organised against Portuguese controls. Equally significant was the resistance staged by merchant chiefs operating from territorial bases along the coast for they put forward their own claims to maritime control and used the agency of the trading permit or cartaz to articulate counter-claims over the sea. The cartaz thus became the new basis for a coastal order that coalesced in the seventeenth century and developed more fully in the eighteenth century.

The resistance of the Malabari corsairs spent itself out in course of the seventeenth century, particularly after the execution of the Marakkar chief in 1600 who had spearheaded the resistance. Fifty years later, Francois Martin, the French traveller, found their power considerably reduced. 'The pirates have at present lost much of their old reputation and their forces have been greatly reduced. They do not have proper territory of their own but are given shelter in the ports of several genteel princes of this coast in return for a share in the proceeds of piracy.'

The Bengal Experience

It is in the folk annals and ballads of Bengal that the impact of the Portuguese on local coastal society finds its most resonant expression. This at first sight appears somewhat incongruous in view of the recent historical researches that have emphasised the marginality of the Portuguese presence in Bengal. Notwithstanding unofficial Portuguese contacts made by traders and deserted soldiers, it was not before

1516 that an official Portuguese expedition was given the responsibility of discovering the Bay of Bengal and its principal ports, Chittagong and Satgaon. The stationing of a fleet in Chittagong to oversee the Carreia de Bengala and the issuing of cartazes was short-lived. In fact, the Portuguese presence was articulated through the Conçession System introduced in the 1660s. Under this arrangement, persons in return for service to the Crown were given in lieu of salary payments, trading concessions to undertake a voyage between any two points in the Indian Ocean. These voyages could be employed in their own shipping. Concessions were of two kinds: in one set of ports, the concessionary was not given the exclusive right to make the voyage but was instead given the position of Captain Major of the fleet from the specified point of departure to that of destination. The position carried with it the monopoly privileges of buying and selling and prior rights of loading and unloading. In another set of ports, the so-called reserve ports, the concessionary secured the exclusive right to trade over a particular commercial port. The concessionaires represented the authority of Goa in Bengal, but in fact, their operations did not affect the fortunes of local ship-owning merchants. Pyrard also suggested that the trade between Bengal and the Maldives was not substantially affected. References to Asian owned shipping from Chittagong to Calicut, from Bengal to Acheh and Bantam have been noted, all of which strongly suggest that shippers were prepared to run the risk of Portuguese intervention. On the Bengal-Gujarat trade and the traffic with the Red Sea, however, there was substantial modification and contraction of trading contacts.

The fragility of the Portuguese presence in Bengal did not, however, spare the small-time trader and seafarer the violence and savagery of the Portuguese encounter. The multiple dimensions of the encounter come out most graphically in the ballads of Eastern Bengal. For the local seafarer, the Portuguese aggression at sea was a fact of enduring reality that had to be borne with courage and tact. The encounter was not limited to the seas; nor was it only a contest for freedom to navigate. Inter-marriages and residence in coastal stations were instrumental in the formation of a hybrid Eurasian community while the inclusion of Portuguese words in the Bengali language and lexicon testified to the vitality and multiple dimensions of the encounter. The earliest references to the word *Phirangi* and *Harmad* occurs in the Bengali poet Mukunda Ram's poem of 1577, wherein he wrote of the intimidating presence of the hated foreigner, the *Harmad* (derived from the Portuguese 'armada').

Chittagong, as mentioned earlier, was the principal port of the Portuguese. In spite of its nominal conquest in Akbar's times, it remained independent. The Arakan kings laid claims to Chittagong; when Peter Mundy wrote his account in 1628-34, it was under Arakan. The Mughals conquered it once again in 1665 and renamed it Islamabad. The Portuguese took full advantage of Chittagong's fluid political status, entered into an alliance with the Maghs (the seafaring inhabitants of Arakan) who had developed a reputation as savage freebooters of the sea. Their destructive raids resulted in large scale depopulation. Bernier mentioned this as he wrote, 'there can be no doubt that the constant terror of attack must have driven away many settlers from the coast even if the numbers killed and enslaved were not sufficient to make so great an impression.' Further, it was widely held that the Portuguese inter-married with local population and thereafter staked claims to territoriality declaring, as Jamini Mohan Ghosh commented, 'our salary was the Indian domain and the whole of Bengal was our jagir.'

Mention is also made by Jamini Mohan Ghosh of the exploits of Sebastien Gonsalves, a Portuguese adventurer who made his initial fortunes in the deltaic trade in salt and set up his centre at Sandwip and double-crossed both the Mughals as well as the Arakanese. Operating closely with the Maghs, the Portuguese plied the seas with reckless audacity and trafficked in slaves with impunity. Manrique referred in this connection to the purchase of slaves from the Maghs at Pipli who were then taken in ships for sale. *The East India Chronicle* reported that in February 1717, the Maghs carried off from the southern part of Bengal, one thousand eight hundred men and women and took them to the kingdom of Arakan where the king chose all the handicraftsmen and about a fourth of the rest for himself and returned the rest of them to be sold into slavery.

The abduction of women by the Maghs and Firangis was followed by loss of caste, an occurrence which, even if predictable, was elaborated by local genealogies or *kula punjis*. D.N. Bhattacharya, in his research on Magh tainted families, referred to the flight of several notables fearing the atrocities of the Portuguese:

> *Krishna Chandrer Bandarer, Paiyea Firingir Dar*
> *Kathaltala Kari Parihar*
> (Krishnachandra fled from Kathaltala in fear of Firingis.)

The Eastern Bengal ballads are even more vivid in their description of the Harmad—Magh menace and the trail of destruction, slavery and mutilation left behind by their raids. The ballad of *Nuranneha and the Grave* is especially evocative as it conjures up the image of the native craft—the Godhu and Ballam (boats carrying rice) threading their way through the Bay where the dreaded Harmads constantly hovered around waiting for an opportunity to pursue them and plunder them of their valuables. 'Swift are the small boats of the pirates which pass over the Bay like birds over the sky,' sang the ballads which describe the Harmads as desperate people who were capable of unflinching courage and daring.

The trials and tribulations of the star-crossed lovers, Nur and Malek at the hands of the Portuguese reveal all too clearly the impression that the Portuguese presence posed an ever present danger to Bengal's coastal society. Enslavement, loss of property and the all-pervasive threat to life were the grim prospects that faced the ordinary seafarer pitched against the Portuguese. The ballad of Nasar Malum is another instance that highlights the trauma of the Portuguese presence as it was recorded and indeed preserved in local memory. The encounter was marked by conflict, blood and gore, loss of caste and occupation. The following excerpt is an interesting instance of how popular ballads such as *Nuranneha* and *Nasar Malum* preserved the memory of the encounter.

'The Harmads were seen at a distance busy observing their ship with the help of telescopes. Nasar felt a shudder at the sight of the miscreants. Ten or twelve of them, dressed in black trousers approached Nasar. Some of them wore red coats and turbans on their heads. In the belt of their waists, they had scabbards bound tightly and they had guns in their hands. The blood flowing the veins of Nasar became frozen in fear. The captains and sailors found their limbs paralysed and could not move their hands and feet. The first thing that robbers did was to hold Nasar tightly by the neck. They slapped his cheeks and the blows were so sudden and severe that Nasar fell down the deck. His sailors and other men lay more like dead than living beings viewing with their timid eyes the action of the robbers.'

Two things emerge from this extract; the obvious naval and technological skills the Portuguese possessed in relation to local seafarers and the dread their presence created. Local seafarers were clearly out of depth in their encounters with the firingi whose activities were seen as not merely damaging but immoral. They were robbers who scoured the seas and preyed on the lawful seafarers whose only option was abject submission. This memory was an enduring one even if it did not correctly represent the fact of Bengali shipping and trade persisting in the sixteenth century. Merchant shipping came to apprehend the Portuguese presence. They travelled in large groups, 'the sloops in those days went in a body—a good number of them together, all compact, when they had to travel a long distance by sea.'

The reputation of the Portuguese as notorious slave drivers was continually reinforced in the subsequent decades. Khafi Khan, author of the *Muntakhab ul Lubab*, referred to their vexatious practice as 'they harassed travellers and exerted themselves continually to strengthen their settlement. Of all the odious practices, this was the worst; in the ports which they occupied on the west coast, they offered no injury either to the property or person of either Mohammedans or Hindus who dwelt upon their rule, but if one of these inhabitants died, leaving children of tender age, they took both the children and the property under their charge, and whether these young people were Saiyids or whether they were Brahmans, they made them Christians and slaves (Mamluk) in the ports of the Konkan in the Dakhin and on the sea coast wherever they had forts and exercised authority, this was the custom of that insolent people.'

Conversions and Local Society

The Portuguese presence had more than one dimension. Khafi Khan who had deplored their proselytising zeal was appreciative of the opportunities that the Portuguese presence in the coast generated amongst a section of the local population. 'Notwithstanding the notoriety of this tyrannical practice, Musalmans and Hindus of all tribes went into their settlements in pursuit of a livelihood and took up abode there.' The organisation of the Goan society under the

Portuguese is an instance in point. Here, conversions, mixed marriages and Portuguese investment resulted in the emergence and growth of a native Christian community whose presence was not marginal. Van Linschoten noted the proliferation of native Christians in and around Goa: 'the countrymen in the villages around Goa and such as labour and till the land are Christians.' This, however, had not affected a change in either their rituals or practices. 'There is not much change,' he observed, 'from the other heathens, for they can hardly leave their heathenish superstitions.' Not surprisingly, therefore, Indian Christian women for the most part remained confined to their homes and when they did venture out, they saw to it that they, 'were not to be seene, for they are carried in a pallamkin covered with a mat or cloth, so that they cannot be seene'.

The prosperity of Goa is well documented. The Portuguese authorities seem to have actually encouraged merchants and seafarers of all nationalities to conduct their transactions. Van Linschoten noted with satisfaction that the town accommodated all sorts of diverse nationalities—Indians, Heathens, Jews, Brahmins among other communities. There were, however, restrictions on public worship by Hindus and Muslims: 'in the places where the Portuguese inhabit and govern, it is not permitted unto them to use them openly, neither to any Indian.'

The occupations of seafaring and sailing remained in the hands of the locals in Goa. They were recruited by the Portuguese themselves thanks to their reputation as excellent seamen. They were organised under a Muqaddam or headman who entered into agreements with the ship master on behalf of his group. The agreement specified the wages that the sailing crew were entitled to, the number of crew and other related details. In fact if Van Linschoten is to be believed, the terms of recruitment were distinctly unfavourable. Their wages were pitifully low in addition to the fact that they were ill treated. They were, however, allowed to travel with their wives and children.

The social dimensions of the Portuguese encounter in the southern littoral, in Malabar and in the Coromandel, were significant. Here, conversion was an important factor in building up networks through the organisation of client communities. The emergence of new communities as a result of conversions altered the existing configurations of coastal society. The Paravas of Tamil Nadu are an instance in point. The Paravas were a seafaring and fishing community inhabiting the southern Coromandel coast and chiefly found in the sea port towns of the Tirunelveli district. The community was held together by common fishing traditions and related occupations and adherence to a common temple and deity at Tiruchandur. The community was organised into sub-castes on the basis of occupation; the Velayar engaged in shallow shipping, the Kadayar in open seafaring, the Nulliyar in tank fishing and the Paravas in open sea fishing. These groups operated within their respective jurisdiction and did not encroach on each other's rights. Their special interest was in the realm of pearl fishing. However, with the increasing influence of the Arabs and the opposition of the Kayalars, (a splinter group of the Paravas), the Paravas toyed with the idea of an alliance with the Portuguese, embracing their faith and reconstituting themselves in the process. For the Portuguese, the overtures of the Paravas were not without prospects of gain. They expected to deploy the skills of the Paravas and substantially enhance their own assets and profits in the region's chank and pearl trade.

A delegation of eighty-five Parava elders negotiated an agreement with the Portuguese captain, Per Vaz de Avaral at Cochin who agreed to commit Portuguese military power to the protection and preservation of the corporate economy of the community or *jati*. The Paravas in return promised to embrace the religion of their new patrons. A spate of mass baptisms followed and earned for the Portuguese a substantial client population in the fishery coast. The Paravas secured for themselves retention of their traditional monopoly rights over chank and pearl fishing. Entire Parava settlements—Tuticorin, Vennilar and Punnakayal—were grafted on newly fortified settlements in the Mannar Islands.

Later observers and ethnologists like Thurston expressed their misgivings and reservations about the advantages that accrued to the community from conversion and Portuguese patronage. The community's independence was undermined; in Thurston's words, 'they dwindled thus from having their own chiefs and their own laws into subordination to priests and Portuguese.' The latter kept for themselves the sovereignty at sea, the peal fisheries and the sovereignty over the Paravas. At the same time, the Paravas were relatively free from political interference from the ruling authorities and used the Portuguese connection effectively to control the lucrative trade in pearls and chanks.

The Advent of the North Europeans in the Seventeenth Century

The advent of the North European trading companies in the seventeenth century did not fundamentally dislocate the existing trading networks in the Indian Ocean. The North Europeans were organised in large joint-stock companies and their early encounters with the Portuguese and the ruling Mughal administration sent ripples across the trading waters of the indigenous seafarer and trader. Like the Portuguese, they were interested in spices and calicoes, the procurement of which necessitated the establishment of trading factories inland. Like the Portuguese, again, they employed the pass not so much as a revenue earner as a means of defining their rights and jurisdiction on the high seas and appropriating the right to convey indigenous trade and shipping. The Dutch were partially successful in restricting Asian shipping in South East Asia after the conquest of Malacca in 1641 and the subjugation of the Spice Islands, but their efforts at monopolising the spice trade in the long run proved abortive. The English East India Company, financially and organisationally weaker than the Dutch East India Company, lagged behind the Dutch and for the greater part of the century confined their operations to South Asia, where a number of trading stations on the coast and inland were established.

The Dutch East India Company was founded in 1602, two years after the English East India Company, and put forward its intentions of acquiring Indian calicoes for trading in the Moluccan spice markets. The capture of Amboyna from the Portuguese in 1605 was followed by securing an imperial farman to establish a factory on the Coromandel coast at Masulipatam, and another at Pulicat further south in 1607. In the Coromandel, the Dutch found themselves negotiating with a plethora of contesting claimants who had carved semi-autonomous fiefs in the wake of the decline of the empire of Vijaynagar. It was only in and after the 1640s, that a semblance of centralisation reappeared in the region when the Qutbshahis of Golconda emerged supreme in central and eastern Dacca and extended their control over large areas of the Coromandel coast stretching from Srikakulam in the north to the Palar river in the south. The southern part of the coast remained under the control of the Nayak of Tanjore, the Thevar of Ramnad and the Nayak of Madura all of whom claimed to be the heirs apparent of Vijaynagar. The fragmented nature of political control along the coast in the first half of the seventeenth century enabled the Dutch to consolidate their hold, establish a number of stations and launch an attack on Portuguese bases to the satisfaction of the ruling Nayaks.

The first Dutch settlements in Bengal were rather late in coming. Besides, the nature of Mughal control precluded the Dutch from enjoying the same concessions and preferential treatment they had secured from the authorities in the Coromandel. Only in 1629, after receiving a permit from the military governor of Pipli, could the VOC establish itself in the region, and that too only on the periphery in Orissa. In 1634, subsequent to the Mughal offensive against the Portuguese at Hughli, the Dutch acquired a farman from Azam Khan, the Subadar of Bengal, which a year later was followed by a second from his successor, Islam Khan, and a third from Shah Jahan, the Mughal emperor himself. These concessions did not, however, include exemption from transit duties, import and export dues. Emboldened by their greater familiarity with the local situation, the Dutch in 1636 stationed a blockading fleet to impede local as well as Portuguese shipping at the mouth of the Ganges. The administration relented and the Dutch position was placed on a firmer footing. A number of factories were established in Balasore, Dacca, Patna, Kasimbazar and Chinsura.

In Western India, the Dutch initiative came after the English had successfully demonstrated their strong-arm methods against Portuguese shipping and the dilatory tactics of the Mughal administration in extending permission to settle down. In 1618, the VOC received its first farman, soon after which a string of factories were opened in Broach, Baroda, Cambay and Ahmedabad in Gujarat proper and in Burhanpur and Agra.

The first decades of the seventeenth century saw the English East India Company locked in a series of naval skirmishes with the Portuguese off Surat. The defeat inflicted by Captain Best in 1612 enabled them to set up shop in Surat and consolidate their affairs. In the Coromandel, they opened factories in Masulipatam in 1611 and a second at Petapuli a year later. In 1640, Fort St. George was founded.

Their initial forays into Bengal were not successful but by 1633, they established two factories in Hariharpur and Balasore and finally obtained in 1651 sanction to share Hughli with the Dutch and the Portuguese. By the 1660s, they began to make some inroads into the Dutch position and even enjoyed the advantage of gaining a virtual exemption from the payment of customs and transit duties in Bengal. This reduced their duties to a mere fortieth part of what the Dutch were obliged to pay. At the same time, there developed a growing consensus among company servants both in India and abroad that their settlements in Bengal would have to be cushioned by fortifications. Job Charnock, more than any other agent realised, in Wilson's words, that, 'treaties could not protect the English trade; he now saw that a fortified station would.' The site chosen was the Sutanuti-Calcutta-Govindpur cluster in 1690 which soon became the bridgehead for English commercial and political expansion.

How were the North Europeans received by indigenous traders and seafarers? Given their record of conflict and contest with the Portuguese in the littoral and with the ruling authorities, Mughal as well as the Sultanates in the Deccan, they could not but be aware of the naval skills and strength the Europeans possessed and could deploy even against the Mughal if they so desired. This effectively raised the value of European protection in the high seas against piracy and the Portuguese themselves. Equally significant was the power of the Mughals on land, a fact that the companies had to take account of in their calculations. What this meant was that all parties concerned—Mughals, Europeans and the local seafaring traders—had to coexist and operate within a system of mutually competing checks and balances. The Mughals on their part knew that their shipping in Gujarat was vulnerable and liable to attacks. The companies on their part knew that their investments in Gujarat as elsewhere were at the mercy of the Mughal State. The actual beneficiary turned out to be the merchant who continued to avail of European convoy services and protection. Notwithstanding the occasional ruptures to commercial ventures in the wake of European aggression off the coast, Indian merchants steadily expanded their overseas operations. Indian shipping registered a phenomenal increase in terms of numbers and tonnage and enjoyed an absolute pre-eminence in the carrying trade of the Ocean. Thus it was not entirely fortuitous that the seventeenth century saw the Indian merchant and seafarer come into his own and successfully negotiate with the Europeans for space in the Indian Ocean. Trade and seafaring expanded substantially benefiting merchants and mariners.

The prosperity of Indian trade and its operators in the seventeenth century derived from the near simultaneous rise of the three empires—Mughal, Ottoman and Safavid—a development which integrated extensive stretches of territory and fostered a network of commercial exchanges. Textiles constituted the single most important export staple, and was absorbed in increasing quantities in the markets of West and South East Asia. The textile trade generated massive inflows of bullion into the Mughal economy which absorbed it and redeployed the same in the form of silver currency. The North Europeans, who had originally entered the markets of the East Indies in search of spices, particularly pepper, were quickly sucked into the trade in calicoes. The organisation of the spice traffic was critically dependent upon the supply of Indian textiles resulting in an expansion of the carrying trade in the Indian Ocean. Europeans participated in increasing numbers in what came to be called the country trade of Asia thus enriching and reinforcing the existing channels of commercial activity. Their operations were adapted and adjusted within the parameters of the existing commercial acumen. While these did not, in any decisive sense, displace existing commercial and maritime networks, it is nonetheless true that littoral societies and indigenous seafaring merchants responded in a particular manner to the interventions that accompanied European enterprise.

The naval strength of the Europeans made a sufficient impression upon indigenous traders who switched over to their dispensation in so far as convoy services in the high seas were concerned. Further, the North European assault on the Portuguese power freed Indian traders of the latter's tribute claims. The Europeans themselves failed to edge out the Indian traders of the carrying trade of the Indian Ocean, with the result that there was a massive expansion of Indian trade and shipping, based mainly on Surat. The ship owners of Surat, mostly Muslims, enjoyed a certain distinction in the city thanks to their links, albeit unofficial, with the ruling administration and their common cultural and religious affiliations. These links enabled them to get the better of the European companies particularly when negotiations revolved around the business of convoy. Merchants like Mulla Abdul Ghafur and Hasan Amadani accused the Europeans of neglecting their obligations and held them to ransom, sometimes successfully with the connivance of the ruling governor. The attempts of the English and Dutch East India Companies to participate in the freight trade of Surat created friction and misunderstandings with the city's Muslim ship owning merchants who persuaded the local administration to intervene on their behalf. In 1644 for instance, we hear of the English factors of Surat complaining against Mirza Mahmud and his 'company of credulous Moors and Bania merchants' who 'have persuaded Mirza Jam Quli Beg, our then Governor, that the English were spreading false scare of French piracy to get Surat freight in their ships'. The local ship owners would appear to have retained control over the city's freight trade until the first quarter of the eighteenth century, when the expansion of European private trade altered the situation considerably.

The Bania merchants whose services were indispensable to the European trade represented additional business for them. The more affluent among them like Virji Vora maintained close connections with the ruling administration. A leading merchant and banker, Vora emerged as the leading merchant of the city by 1625 with access to an enormous capital stock that enabled him to corner spices and pepper to the distinct detriment of the English company. He exploited the rivalry between the Dutch and the English companies to retain his control over the market and over select commodities such as pepper. The English were suitably deferential to Virji's demands; on one occasion, referred to by B.G. Gokhale in his monograph on Surat, when the English captured an Indian junk with Virji's cargo, they quietly restored his goods; they gave their own safe conduct passes to ships sailing out of Surat's harbour only when such action was recommended by Vora. The brokers who attached themselves to the European East India companies, both Parsi and Bania, (the Parakh and Manek families for instance) steadily consolidated their positions to expand their own ventures. The English connection stood them well particularly in the troubled decades of the eighteenth century, when they petitioned the company authorities to take them under their protection and act as a counterpoise to the bankrupt Mughal administration.

The success story of the Indian seafarer and trader in Surat was not an isolated or even exceptional event in the annals of seventeenth century maritime India. Historians have demonstrated how local trading groups in the Coromandel and Bengal prospered in the seventeenth century and substantially expanded their scope of overseas operations. However, the extent of penetration into local coastal society as a result of European initiative tended to be much sharper particularly in the Coromandel. The Parava-Marakkaiyar conflict largely orchestrated through the agency of the Dutch

East India Company is an instance in point, when an existing conflict was shored up by the intervention of the Europeans.

A striking feature of the Coromandel trade in the seventeenth century lay in its eastward orientation. Trade with South East Asia, which had always been the mainstay of the region's commerce peaked in the seventeenth century as Hindu and Muslim shipping frequented the Sumatran, Malayan, Javanese and Moluccan markets with textiles and rice. The trade with the west, despite a slow and sluggish start, picked up in due course as a result of the tie up of the Golconda state with the Islamic world of West Asia. Most of the westward trade originated from Masulipatam which emerged as the premier entrepot of the Coromandel. Like Surat, this port city owed its prosperity to the benefits of political consolidation. The emergence and expansion of the Golconda state with its attendant implications—a larger hinterland and consuming aristocracy—improved Masulipatam's prospects as a trading centre. At the same time, Narsipur emerged as an important ship-building centre supplying a large fleet for the region's merchants. Persian merchants besides local Hindu and Muslim commercial groups thrived under state patronage. This did not imply that the state consistently took up cudgels for their merchants against European pressure. Like the Mughals, the Golconda rulers preferred to deal with the Europeans on land and did not hesitate to work on a compromise formula on matters regarding maritime control and jurisdiction. On the whole, however, the state of Golconda was more receptive to commercial matters partly because of its own investments in overseas trade. This did not substantially alter the fact that everywhere, merchants in Masulipatam or in smaller units such as Ramnad were ultimately dependent on networks of contacts with political authorities of family and community connections to deal with a crisis situation. The efficacy of political connections depended very much on their timing—

if it happened to coincide with the political agenda of the authorities, traders and merchants could expect a cohesive settlement to emerge; if not, they had to settle for a compromise that only partially protected their interests. In areas that were predominantly coastal and where merchants and seafaring groups were closely entrenched in the ruling set up, the encounter with the European companies assumed interesting configurations.

THE SEAFARER'S POLITICS: THE RAMNAD CASE

The Marava State of Ramnad emerged as an independent unit in the second half of the seventeenth century. Initially under the control of the Madura Nayaks, the State of Ramnad under the Marava Setupati secured a measure of autonomy and assumed a distinct maritime profile. The Setupati concentrated his energies in building up substantial commercial and maritime assets for his fledgling state. The cooperation of the Marakkaiyar mercantile community was enlisted in this project, which resulted in a strong maritime coalition coalescing against the Dutch East India Company.

The Dutch interest in the Fishery Coast coincided with their takeover of Ceylon from the Portuguese in 1658. A treaty was concluded in 1660 between Tirumala Setupati of Ramnad and Van Goens of the Dutch Company. Dutch maritime interest in this region centred around the pearl fishing business which was worked by both Parava and Marakkaiyar groups. The special position accorded to the Kilkarai-based Marakkaiyar family of Shaikh al Qadir better known as Peria Tambi, enabled Marakkaiyar interests to combine and mount an offensive against Dutch intervention and their attempted monopoly of pearl fishing and pepper trade across the Pamban Channel to Ceylon. Peria Tambi himself was a full fledged trader engaged in large scale trade with Ceylon, a business that he was able to operate more efficiently on account of his political office. On the other hand, his appointment as tax farmer of the south-western fringes of Ramnad territory brought him into conflict with the Paravas who resisted the newly improved fiscal demands and solicited the Dutch for assistance and arbitration. The Dutch were only too eager to fish in troubled waters hoping thereby to dislodge local Muslim interests from the pearl and pepper traffic.

The scale of Parava and Marakkaiyar investment in the pearl fishery business was substantial. Pearl fishing drew boats from Tuticorin, Kilkarai, Kayalpatnam, Sundarapatnam and Pannaikayal. The Marakkaiyars were prominent in Kilkarai, Kayalpatnam and Sundarapatnam while Tuticorin and Punnaikayal were dominated by the Paravas. Adam Labbai, Peria Tambi Marakkaiyar and Chinna Marakkaiyar figured prominently among Kilkarai's operators. The organisation of the pearl business was complicated involving a miscellany of groups and supervisors—boat owners or *campanottis* who had to advance money to the divers; the divers themselves who were attached to the one or the other of the boat owners.

The Dutch-Marakkaiyar confrontation broke out over the issue of control of the pearl fishery. In 1698, when the Dutch announced that a pearl fishery was to be set afoot, their peons were physically abused by the Marakkaiyar officials. A strongly worded protest was lodged with the Setupati who agreed to rebuke and fine the guilty officials. This, as it turned out, was a charade for the Dutch found, themselves in an unenviable situation when the pearl fishery was actually sabotaged by the Marakkaiyar notables. By late February 1698, the Dutch factors at Tuticorin complained that Muslim boat owners were refusing to advance money to the pearl divers. As it happened, the pearl fishery of March-April 1698 turned out to be a complete fiasco. Divers barely showed up and the operations came to a grinding halt. Local divers and fishers chafed against the restrictions that the Dutch initiated. For instance, the Dutch insisted on seafarers registering themselves under the Dutch settlement giving details of owners' names, description of the boats and a written promise to sell the proceeds of the fishery to select merchants in Tuticorin and Kayalpatnam. These regulations introduced a measure of control that the local seafarers were unaccustomed to. They were persuaded by men like Peria Tambi to oppose them and go on a general strike. The strike of 1698 that followed was a success and compelled the Dutch to step down and to contemplate more amicable means of neutralising Marakkaiyar opposition by enlisting the cooperation of Peria Tambi himself.

The volte face, however, yielded only temporary dividends. Neither the Ramnad ruler nor his Marakkaiyar clients were prepared to tow the Dutch line indefinitely, particularly over the contentious issue of controlling the Pamban Channel. The Dutch, anxious to restrict access to Asian and European shipping, resented Peria Tambi's manipulations. Resistance continued well into the first decades of the eighteenth century when the Ramnad State, bedevilled with financial problems, could no longer sustain the anti-Dutch offensive.

Elsewhere too, seafarers were able to hold their own against the European factor. It must be remembered that European trading companies were unable to displace indigenous mercantile networks that dominated the sea lanes of the Indian Ocean. In port cities like Surat and Hugli, Asian shipping held a distinct edge over European shipping despite the ubiquity of the European trading permit. Merchants and rulers alike accepted the necessity of utilising European convoy services in the Indian Ocean and endorsing the validity of the European pass. This did not seriously undermine the strength of their ventures; in Surat, as we have seen, merchants were able to turn convoy agreements on their head and extract considerable advantages from the

Europeans. Merchants like Hasan Amadani and Abdul Ghafur rarely failed to get the better of the European companies by skilfully employing their connections with the Durbar. Thus, after the initial forays over the aggression of the hat wearers had died down, Indian merchants settled down to the all important business of making money from trade. Also, European settlements generated new opportunities for coastal groups and mercantile castes and enabled the latter to acquire greater social mobility. The process of accommodation was not necessarily or always smooth—the annals of Bengal and Malabar transmit all too vividly the divisive aspect of the Portuguese intervention in coastal society. The merchant, the boatman and the fisher had to come to grips with a new political reality, namely, that the sea they had so long plied was no longer a free realm. On the other hand, the encounter between the Indians and Europeans did not, until the eighteenth century, deflect the trajectory of indigenous mercantile enterprise. The success and ramifications of Indian mercantile activity struck the Europeans forcefully as they jostled with them for space and returns.

The eighteenth century ushered in even more fundamental changes as the politics of transition gave way to a more settled order under the hegemony of the English East India Company. Everywhere along the coast, there was an attempt to break out from the confines of the existing order enforced by a variety of potentates, namely the Sidi, the Angria and the European East India companies. There was a perceptible loosening of the order in the course of the first half of the eighteenth century particularly in the Gujarat and Konkan coast, where local chiefs of Maratha extraction challenged the authority of the waning Mughal as well as the English East India Company. The reordering of coastal politics under the dispensation of the English East India Company significantly altered the face of coastal society. While the new order impinged directly on the seafarers forcing them to accept passes before embarking on their voyages, it also generated a wide range of opportunities for employment. Seafarers were encouraged to take up residence in the growing English enclaves of Bombay, Madras and Calcutta. In Bombay, for instance, local fishermen were allotted dwellings and at a later stage, even markets were organised to ensure regular fish stocks to the city. Under the stewardship of Gerald Aungier, efforts were stepped up to encourage new settlers to take up residence in the island city. In the words of James Douglas, an English observer of the nineteenth century, 'We did everything we could to induce wealthy natives to settle on it, and whenever they were to be found in Kachh, nay even on the coasts of the Persian Gulf and Red Sea, our ships were told to give the immigrants a free passage to the island of Bombay.' The policy paid dividends as a range of mercantile men from the enterprising shipwright to the humble Koli fisher flocked into the city to make a living. Mercantile castes like the Gujarati Bania and the Navayat Muslim made their way in search of new pastures and profits and initiated a new stage in Indo-European partnership. The process of accommodation between the new power, the English East India Company, and local coastal society varied from region to region. It is to this story of accommodation amidst apocalypse that we now turn our attention to.

Notes and References

Most of the material used in this chapter has been drawn from a variety of well known publications on India's maritime trade in the sixteenth and seventeenth centuries. These include Ashin Dasgupta, *Indian Merchants and the Decline of Surat 1700-1750*, (Franz Verlag, Wiesbaden, 1979), M.N. Pearson, *Merchants and Rulers in Gujarat: The Response to the Portuguese in the Sixteenth Century* (Manohar, 1979), S. Arasaratnam, *Maritime India in the Seventeenth Century* (New Delhi, 1994), Sanjay Subrahmanyam, *Improvising Empire: Portuguese Trade and Settlement in the Bay of Bengal 1500-1700* (Delhi, 1990), *The Political Economy of Commerce, Southern India 1500-1650* (Cambridge, 1990), Om Prakash, *The Dutch East India Company and the Economy of Bengal* (Princeton, 1984). Dr. Ashin Dasgupta's publications have been particularly illuminating in reconstructing the story of Indian seafaring merchants in the first half of the eighteenth century. Charles Boxer's *The Portuguese Seaborne Empire 1415-1815* (Hutchinson, 1969) is a classic and strongly hints at the complexity of the Indo-European encounter.

For Bengal, extensive use has been made of Jamini Mohan Ghosh, *Magh Raiders in Bengal* (Calcutta, 1960) and *The Eastern Bengal Ballads Vol. IV Part I*, compiled and edited by Dinesh Chandra Sen, (University of Calcutta, 1932). Both these publications offer alternative perceptions of the Portuguese impact on local society. The story of the Paravas and the Marakkaiyars has been pieced together from V.N. Rao, David Schulman and Sanjay Subrahmanyam, *Symbols of Substance: Court and State in Nayaka Period Tamil Nadu* (Delhi, 1992) and Patrick a Roche, *Fisherman of the Coromandel: The Social Study of the Parravas of the Coromandel* (Delhi, 1984). Also see Sanjay Subrahmanyam, 'Noble Harvest from the Sea: Managing the Pearl Fishery of Mannar, 1500-1925' in *Institutions and Economic Change in South Asia,* (ed.) Burton Stein and Sanjay Subrahmanyam, (Delhi, 1996).

Among the travel accounts that have been used, mention must be made of Taboys Wheeler (ed.) *Early Travels in India: Reprints of Rare and Curious Narratives of Old Travellers in India in the Sixteenth and Seventeenth Centuries* (Reprint, 1994), Francois Martin, *Travels in Africa, Persia and India 1664-1670*, translated and edited by Aniruddha Ray (Calcutta, 1990).

For Persian histories and impressions, see the *History of India as Told by Its Own Historians* edited and translated by Sir H. M. Elliot and J. Dowson, (London, 1866). Also see Zayn al-Din, *Tuhhfat al Mujahadin* translated by S. Muhammad Husayn Nainar (University of Madras, 1942). Both Stephen Frederic Dale, *The Mapillas of Malabar 1498-1922* (Oxford, 1980) and Genevieve Bouchon's *Regent of the Seas: Cannanore's Response to Portuguese Expansion 1507-1522* (Delhi, 1988) are extremely informative about the Portuguese encounter in Malabar.

Indian Seafarers in the Eighteenth Century: The Parting of Ways

The crisis of the eighteenth century and its attendant implications on Indian society and economy have formed the subject of extensive research. Recent studies focusing on the nature and workings of the successor regimes of the eighteenth century have tended, by and large, to locate elements of growth in the regional economies the new rulers controlled. The successful organisation of regional political regimes and the marshalling of revenue for the same constituted an important marker of growth and vitality. The profile and orientation of the new regimes was not exclusively agrarian; we do have instances of rulers like Martanda Varma of Travancore and Tipu Sultan of Mysore attempting to control and tax overseas trade and in the process locking horns with the European East Indian companies. Nevertheless, recent historiography on the eighteenth century has passed over the issues of maritime politics and control with the result that the story of the sea and its changing political configurations in this century has remained unsaid. The omission is surprising in view of the fact that the rise and assertion of the new power and a sea power at that, namely the English East India Company, put paid to the aspirations of the regional states and decisively redrew the political map of Hindustan and its littoral. Also, there is a clearly stated consensus that the developments in the eighteenth century irreparably dislocated the trading structure of maritime India and reduced Indian shippers and seafarers to a position of subordination. Indeed, the casualties of the eighteenth century crisis were the shippers and seafaring merchants who found their way blocked by the looming presence of the European fleet in the Indian waters. For us to situate the Indian seafarer in a new and altered context of company hegemony, we need first of all to delineate the discrete elements that made up the 'eighteenth century crisis' as it was perceived by the Indian seafarer and trader and to locate thereafter his attempts to deal with the same.

The Crisis of the Eighteenth Century

The greater part of the eighteenth century represented a period of political contraction and economic decline for the trading world of maritime India. Barring the region of Bengal, which under the stewardship of Murshid Quli Khan and his successors enjoyed the benefits of political security and accelerated economic growth in the first half of the eighteenth century, the other parts of the Mughal Empire fell prey to the inexorable pressures of Mughal decline. Imperial authority was contested everywhere and at every level leaving the trader bereft of any security. Of all the regions, western India and more specifically Gujarat sustained the most severe reverses. Here, as Ashin Dasgupta has demonstrated, the crisis of Mughal decline was double-edged. It manifested itself in myriad forms: the collapse of the local administration in the face of ruthless assaults by the Marathas, the greatest opponents of the empire; financial bankruptcy leaving the local governors to resort to arbitrary action against their merchants; the isolation of Gujarati towns and commercial centres like Surat and their detachment from the larger hinterland which had sustained their commerce and finally, the beginnings of a tentative offensive on the part of the European East India companies to press for additional commercial and fiscal privileges. The tragedy of Mughal decline was most strikingly played out in Surat, the Bandar Mubarak. Here, the local administration was subject to a series of devastating blows by the Marathas who in the course of their military operations severed the city's links with the rest of the sub-continent. This meant that the city merchants could no longer draw their supplies from the larger hinterland of northern India or, for that matter, market their imports. Movement of money through hundis was interrupted rendering all long distance commercial operations extremely hazardous. Worse still, the occupation of the Athavisi, the twenty-eight villages adjacent to Surat, by the Marathas in the 1730s denuded the ruling administration of its principal source of revenue. Under the circumstances, the local administration with its back to the wall, took recourse to the strategy of mercantile taxation. Merchants were subject to a series of dues and exactions.

The timing could not have been worse. The simultaneous decline of the Ottoman and Safavid empires threw the markets in West Asia into disarray. Conditions of trade in the high seas deteriorated as piratical attacks increased in scale and incidence. Thus merchants and shippers were compelled to restrict their sphere of operations. At the same time, they had to compete with the traffic of the English private traders of Bombay and Surat in the carrying trade of the western Indian Ocean. This had more than one implication: the expansion of European trade, private as well as corporate, represented an unwelcome competition which the Indian merchant could barely hope to withstand. At another level, the expansion had an implicit political overtone, for it was only a matter of time before the Company began to contemplate schemes for greater political and commercial control. The Company's interest in the freight trade was at variance with the material interests of the local seafaring trader who could hardly hope to count on the support of the ruling administration. The merchants of Surat led by the redoubtable Mulla Muhammad Ali staged a rebellion against the ruling governor protesting against arbitrary taxation and even got him replaced by another claimant whom they mistakenly assumed to be a safe choice. What they failed to realise was that change of personalities could not deflect the inexorable course of decline or that an even greater threat to their interests was the English East India Company. Admittedly, Muslim shipowners like the Chellaby family or that of Mulla Muhammad Ali were by no means oblivious to the growing threat of the English company and even resisted for a while the attempts of the city's Bania leader Seth Laldas Jagannath to co-opt the English company into the protest movement. They held out till as late as 1759 but to no avail.

The company's political project in western India remained somewhat limited and tentative for the greater part of the first half of the eighteenth century. Essentially, their schemes until the 1740s revolved around the issue of coastal and maritime control, preconditions to which were the acquisition of the Imperial Admiralty held by the Sidi, and the enforcement of the company's trading permit along the entire stretch of the littoral. Every seafarer from Sind in the north to Malabar in the south was obliged to avail of the company's pass. Implicit in the acceptance of the pass was a restructuring of politics in the high seas as well as the imposition of controls and a new fiscal structure on the region's seafarers and traders. All seafaring traders had to apply for the company's pass which defined the sovereign rights of the company to police and patrol the high seas. Navigation was no longer a right to be exercised freely by the seafarer; he had to seek the sanction of the company to do so and in return was guaranteed protection by the company against the claims of other potentates. Notwithstanding the benefits of company protection, the imposition of the pass and its rigid enforcement by the guns of the Bombay Marine, the naval arm of the company establishment in western India, implied a set of controls that negated the claims of existing coastal powers. Under the circumstances, the interaction between local coastal society, its seafarers and rulers and the English East India Company was bound to be tense and violent.

Development in other maritime regions, notably Bengal, did not quite follow the same trajectory. The port of Hugli, the principal outlet of Bengal's seaborne trade, enjoyed preeminence until the 1720s attracting a considerable volume of commerce to its roadsteads. Besides, the increasing investment of the European East India companies injected considerable quantities of bullion into the economy. Indigenous enterprise, however, was hit by the steady growth of English private trade that encroached upon the fortunes of the local seafaring merchant. Also, the decline of Surat and the Gujarati-West Asia connection could not but affect Bengal's export trade to the markets of the Arabian and Persian Gulfs. Company officials had occasion to comment on the steady decline that set in in the Surat-Murshidabad traffic which involved exchange of silk and cotton. Thus by the 1740s, the fortunes of Hugli dwindled—a process that was directly related to the dislocation of trading networks within the Indian sub-continent as well as to the Maratha raids that temporarily dislocated the economy of Bengal, particularly in its western districts. The decline of Gujarati shipping was followed by the rise of Calcutta and the phenomenal expansion of English country trade in the markets of West Asia. Even though English connection with West Asia was short-lived—by the 1760s, for instance, English shipping turned increasingly towards China—the competition of English private trade had serious implications for local commercial interests in Bengal. Muslim shipping staged a quiet retreat as the ships of the English established sole control over the region's freight traffic. Non-shipowning merchants of Hindu/Bania extraction switched over to the English carriage services, their choice being dictated by material considerations of greater security. The English ships, P.J. Marshall suggests, had developed a reputation for being seaworthy and capable of withstanding piratical attacks on the high seas, a factor that prompted Gujarati merchants resident in Bengal to use their ships for trade and transportation.

Politics in the Coromandel was characterised by a measure of fluidity even as early as the latter decades of the seventeenth century. The decay of the Deccan Sultanates and their incorporation by the Mughal state, the subsequent decline of Mughal authority in the wake of the Maratha counter-offensive in the first decades of the eighteenth century and the assertion of regional independence by erstwhile Mughal potentates like the Nizam of Hyderabad and the Nawab of Arcot resulted in conditions of chronic political insecurity. Existing channels of commercial and productive activity were dislocated as merchants and weavers faced uncertainty, political unrest, rising costs of food grains and raw materials. Masulipatam lost its position as the chief importer of South East Asian and West Asian goods for the region. The interrupted communication between Masulipatam and the new Mughal centre of Hyderabad was never adequately restored; furthermore, the newly appointed governor of Masulipatam was quick to exploit his position and the fluid nature of contemporary politics to enhance collection of customs duties and inland transit dues. This resulted in a dispersal of merchants away from Masulipatam which by 1738 resembled a ghost town. Merchants migrated to other centres like Madras and San Thome which enjoyed the patronage of the Nawab of Arcot and for a while emerged as a major trading outlet in the Coromandel. The trade of the European companies in the Coromandel suffered, according to S. Arasaratnam, major reverses in the first decades of the eighteenth century when political unrest impeded regular supplies.

Conditions of political insecurity and unrest eroded the very basis of trade affecting all merchants, Indians and Europeans alike. The European factors with their dubashes were unanimous in condemning the anarchy that had overtaken the realm. Ananda Ranga Pillai, Dupleix's dubash in Pondicherry, echoed the spirit of the times when he wrote with characteristic elegance, 'In times of decay, order disappears giving place to disorder and justice to injustice. Men no longer observe their caste rules but transgress their bounds so that castes are confused and force governs.' It was only after the 1720s that the situation began to show signs of improvement in the company enclaves. Madras emerged as an important port of call where European merchants in partnership with Indian agents conducted extensive sailings towards South East Asia. Long distance coastal trade took ships to Bengal. Arasaratnam has suggested that Indian traders benefited from the rise of the English settlement and that even those Madras merchants who had dealt with the English as middlemen pursued their overseas shipping interests. Hindu shipping became visible; ships called Venkaṭesh, Tirupathy, Veerabhadra, Venkatalatchumi and Arunachalam plied the seas. Their owners were Komaties, Balija Chetties, Beri Chetties or Vyapari Chetties. Muslim shipping also persisted but the base of their operations remained San Thome and Porto Novo where the Chulias held forth. In fact more recent work suggests that Chulia enterprise continued right through the greater part of the eighteenth century and that its ramifications have not yet been properly evaluated.

The one thing that emerges from the discourses of decline is the impact of 'conflict' (the participants ranging from the Mughal to the Maratha to the European private trader) on the trading order that sustained overseas trade and commerce. Political authority was being contested at various levels and this could not but engender conditions of chronic insecurity and impede the movement of traffic and vital supplies. The operations of merchants suffered dislocation and the options left to them were strictly limited. Migration to adjacent centres was one. The other was to accept the protection of the European East India companies, settle down in their fortified enclaves and trade within their jurisdiction. This was not necessarily a bad bargain but over time, the parity of the Indian seafarer and merchant with his European counterpart was deliberately undermined following the acquisition of political power by the English East India Company. The steady intrusion of private European trading interests into the commercial and political networks of maritime India eroded the autonomy of the Indian merchant and provided the English company with a definite agenda for control. The expansion of the company directly impinged upon local coastal society which was among the first to register its responses to the new politics of the eighteenth century.

Politics in the West Coast

The disintegration of Mughal authority along the west coast, particularly in the Gujarat littoral, was not evident until the 1720s and 1730s, when major changes occurred within the existing political set up. Significant among these were the region's isolation from the centre and the larger hinterland, and the physical occupation of parts of the suba by the Marathas. This put pressure on the faction ridden Mughal bureaucracy, which, in a desperate drive for funds turned to the merchants. Everywhere, in Cambay, Ahmedabad and

Surat, the ruling Mughal administration singled out local merchants for financial 'assistance'. The merchants on their part, anxious to salvage what remained of their flagging ventures, turned to the European East India companies for protection against the arbitrary Mughal officials as well as the unpredictable Maratha intruder. The onus fell principally upon the English company stationed at Surat and Bombay to assume the role of 'protector of the free trader', a role that eminently fitted into their own commercial interests. In fact, at this stage, the company's interests were focused on the office of the Imperial Admiralty which would enable them to enforce absolute control over the seas through the medium of the pass. Coastal and maritime hegemony thus figured significantly in the political agenda of the English East India Company.

The company was, however, not the only contender for maritime control. The decline of Mughal authority encouraged local potentates along the coast to assert their autonomy and articulate their claims on the littoral and high seas. This tendency was particularly marked in the Konkan coast which, even in the seventeenth century, had not enjoyed the benefits of centralised political control. Important Deshmukh families like the Desais of Savantwadi, the Surves of Shringapur, the Malwans of Sindhudurg and the Shirkes of Kutre all of whom had been subdued by Shivaji and subsequently by the Mughal subadar of the Konkan, resumed their political game. The Angrias of Kolaba under Kanhoji Angria were particularly active and maintained a strict vigil over all vessels sailing along the coast. Kanhoji's fleet consisted of eight or ten gallivats but this was more than made up for by his prowess and daring. He derived his authority from the larger Maratha government and exercised his power in the name of his sovereign. S.N. Sen suggests that Kanhoji's politics did not in any significant way differ from that of the Portuguese, the English or the Dutch, all of whom claimed the exclusive right to police the seas and establish the authority of their trading permit as the only legitimate one. Kanhoji's claims were disputed by other contenders, including the English company. The result was a further loosening of the political system along the coast rendering the operations of the seafarer extremely hazardous.

The Angria fleet was a terror which the seafarers were glad to avoid at all costs. Merchants and seafaring communities who had flocked into Bombay in search of safe pastures, fell back on the company's protection. The company on its part, was unwilling to relinquish its rights and jurisdiction over the seas and therefore, entered into a prolonged conflict with Kanhoji and his successors thereafter. The war lasted nearly thirty-eight years and finally ended in favour of the English. In fact, right through the 1740s and 1750s, the company's naval establishment, the Bombay Marine, fought intermittently for control of the seas against a number of contenders—the Angrias, the Malwans, the Sidis of Janjira and the Desais of Savantwadi—all of whom were dubbed as pirates and whose activities were detrimental to the fair trader. The rhetoric of the fair trader whose protection the company had magnanimously assumed responsibility for was backed by the guns of the Marine. The strategy was effective and persuaded a substantial section of seafaring society to switch over to the English system of control.

The altercations between the English company and the coastal rulers centred around two principal issues, namely the political scope of the pass and the extent of the English settlement's (Bombay's) jurisdiction. As far as the company was concerned, the successful enforcement of their cartaz legitimised their control over the seas and littoral and its trade and shipping. Merchants accepting the pass were assured of diplomatic immunity and protection against attacks of rival powers on the high seas. This was, however, technically speaking not admissible; the pass of one maritime power was not regarded as a legal protection against the aggression of another, and exemption from this obligation could be obtained only by convention or treaty. What made the English assurance different and effective was the fact that the company undertook military action on an extensive scale in defence of their protege merchants right through the 1740s and 1750s.

The mid-century victories of 1759 and 1765 against the Angrias and Malwans of Sindhudrug respectively enhanced the credentials of the English East India Company as a leading maritime power on the west coast of India. This encouraged the company to articulate a new system of controls along the littoral, a system which was novel in its organisation if not in conception and quite unlike that of the other territorial powers along the coast. The company's power assumed a disembodied form of control over all traffic on the high seas and jurisdiction over all seafarers and merchants. The authority of the English pass was pronounced sacrosanct and guaranteed its owner immunity from the attacks of rivals. By the end of the century, all seafaring inhabitants came under the ambit of the company's cartaz and the issue of passes became a systematised procedure.

How did local coastal society in Gujarat and the Konkan respond to these developments? Did the success and assertion of company politics spell unmitigated disaster for the region's seafaring and trading communities or were they able to perceive added advantages under the new dispensation? Even a cursory examination of company records or for that matter of the merchant migrations into Bombay suggests that a good measure of ambivalence characterised the initial responses of local seafarers, many of whom came to recognise the benefits of the monopoly pass system instituted by the company. The reluctance of local seafarers and traders to accept the company's controls gave way to guarded enthusiasm particularly after the decisive victories over the Angrias and Malvans, the facilities offered by Bombay in terms of diplomatic protection, preferential custom rates and political security. These encouraged a miscellany of seafaring groups—traders, fishermen and sailors—to take up residence in the island city of Bombay and conform to the new order under the dispensation of the English company. S.M. Edwardes refers in this connection to the influx of the Navayats into Bombay and their amalgamation into the so called Konkani Muslim community. Other communities like the Parsis, Bohras and Hindu Banias of Gujarati and Marwari origin also responded to the overtures of the company which was anxious to people the new city with service groups whose skills could be satisfactorily deployed to the advantage of its own trading interests. The new residents were therefore, particularly welcome if their activities corresponded to the company's commercial interests, private as well as corporate. Parsis for instance, flocked to the Bombay shipyard as ship builders and worked very closely with European merchants in the capacity of partners in export trade and shipping. The case of Jardine Matheson working with Jamsetjee Jeejeebhoy is a case in point. The Mayor's Court Registers carry extensive references to the early joint ventures of the Bombay merchants, Konkanis, Gujaratis and Parsis, all of which add up to the fact that the rise of the new city and the enforcement of the new order was taken ample advantage of by local seafaring and commercial groups. The first batch of Gujarati Bania migrants set up *kothis* in Bombay and handled money-lending operations on an extensive scale. They were involved in the insurance and respondentia business and operated the important business of Hundi transfers between Bombay and the major credit centres of Hindustan and western India. With the rise of the China trade in the latter decades of the eighteenth century, they became suppliers of raw cotton besides financing the trade in the commodity.

The Parsi merchants of Bombay along with the European agency houses handled the export trade in cotton and later opium, consigning the staple on their own ships. They became ardent advocates of company expansion along the Gujarat littoral arguing that the movement of cotton was impeded by the destabilising presence of the Marathas in the region and by the activities of semi-piratical groups along the Gujarat-Kathiawad coasts. As beneficiaries of the new dispensation, they clamoured for organisation of better convoy services and the suppression of piracy along the Gujarat-Kathiawad littoral. The company, however, did not wrest the initiative until the turn of the nineteenth century, when efforts were redoubled to dislodge the piratical chieftains of Okha Mandal and Beyt Dwarka.

The Bombay settlement for the greater part of the eighteenth century was perceived as an alternative trading centre by regional commercial groups, many of whom adapted to the new colonial system that accompanied the establishment of British paramountcy in Hindustan. For the ordinary seafarer, who pursued his livelihood in the capacity of sailor or fisher, residence in Bombay was not initially an unattractive proposition. The community of Koli fishermen, for example, settled down within the ambit of the new system emerging as important suppliers of fish for the new urban centre and its growing residents. A similar case can be made out for the sailors who manned the ships of the English East India Company and the shipwrights who built vessels at the Bombay shipyard. The Wadias established their reputation as the city's most sought after shipwrights. Ordinary sailors continued to man the ships of the European merchants. It was only after the advent of steam-shipping, when new skills were required and when a new hierarchy of power and command was enforced, that indigenous sailors were reduced to the subordinate position of deck hands, stokers and stewards. Their wages were low and terms of recruitment distinctly unfavourable. Local sailors were by and large losers in the new recruitment process initiated by European steamship companies under the colonial regime in the nineteenth century.

Recent researches have located the success and enterprise of local trading groups in western India who managed to drive lucrative channels of commercial traffic outside the strict confines of the colonial trading structure. The Bhatias, Lohanas and Memons from Cutch and Kathiawad as well as the Bohras migrated to Bombay in growing numbers in the nineteenth century and drove a vigorous trade with West Asia and the East African littoral. The case of Tyabjee Bhoymeeah is an instance in point. A Sulaimani Bohra, Bhoymeeah's father came to Bombay in the eighteenth century and set up shop which functioned as a retail outlet for European and Chinese goods. Tyabjee himself worked with the city's Parsi merchants and by the 1860s operated a mercantile firm with an impressive turnover. There were an impressive number of success stories of indigenous enterprise in Bombay—Parsis trading to China, Bhatias to East Africa and Gujarati Banias to Muscat and Zanzibar.

The establishment of the new dispensation coming in the wake of the dislocation of the old trading order claimed a number of casualties particularly in the old port city of Surat, where Muslim shipping interests (Bohra and Sunni) had prevailed for the greater part of the seventeenth and early eighteenth centuries. Bereft of political and institutional security, the Muslim shippers found themselves incapable of competing with the aggressive European trader whose commercial ventures and freight business cut into the dwindling profits of the old *saudagar*. The Castle Revolution of 1759 in Surat, which invested the English East India Company with the office of Qiladar and with extensive powers of arbitration over the ruling administration, helped the English stabilise and consolidate their private trading operations. Most of the English officials combined trade with public office—the Chiefs of the Surat establishment and the Governors of Bombay like William Wake, Thomas Hodges and Thomas Price between 1759 and 1770 exploited their newly achieved political authority to monopolise the city's freight trade to West Asia. They proceeded to systematically prevent local shipowners from participating in the freight business. Protests by local merchants were ineffective. Mulna Fakirodin, great grandson of Mulla Abdul Ghafur in 1774, accused the Surat Chief, Daniel Draper, of unfair practices. In his representation to the Mayor's Court in Bombay, he maintained that 'no freight ships for Mocha or Judda could be put up with any probability of success without their permission and influence'. He also admitted to having entered into an agreement with Daniel Draper on behalf of Thomas Hodges, wherein he agreed to certain conditions and promised to pay Rs. 15,000 for his ship the Fatty Mubarak and Rs. 3,000 for the other provided that they prevented putting up any other ships for freight. Under this informal arrangement, Hodges had also promised to make available English passes and colours for the ships due to sail. None of these arrangements had materialised. In fact, Hodges and Draper had actually allowed vessels belonging to their protege merchants, namely, Manakjee Mody, Govind Jeevan and Shamji Narranset to be put up for freight and proceed to Judda. This wilful violation, Fakirodin argued, had been detrimental to his operations.

Fakirodin's representation reflected all too vividly the constraints and pressures that the city's Muslim traders had to cope with. The English presence in the city buttressed by their occupation of the Surat Castle put pressure on the freight operations of merchants like Mulna Fakirodin and Ahmed Chellaby. Survival depended on private English connections and even these were not foolproof guarantees. The Chellabies had occasion to protest against the company's mismanagement of the freight trade. In 1768, they made use of their influence with the Turkish authorities of Baghdad to complain against the Surat Chief's unfair practices. In 1788, they even persuaded the Court of Directors to enquire into the situation. The result was a series of regulations calculated to restore the freight trade to its previous status and eliminate all undue influence of English officials over its management. In practice, however, these regulations did not make a substantial difference to the Muslim shippers, big or small. The company officials continued to dominate what remained of the languishing freight trade to the Gulfs of Arabia and Persia until the 1790s. The trade to the Gulf did not recover to its pre-1740 levels but even at its reduced scale absorbed more than half the region's textile manufactures. Further the traffic coincided with the annual pilgrimage and accommodated numerous Hajjis.

The enforcement of company controls materially affected the Hajjis. We come across a petition in the 1770s as well as in the 1790s put forward by the merchants of Surat. This petition outlined in detail the difficulties they encountered in their annual voyages (trade and pilgrimage) to the Gulfs on account of the new management of the company. In addition to the high-handedness of the company officials who monopolised the freight trade to their advantage, they compelled the penurious Hajjis to pay passage money, something which they could ill afford to do. 'It is well known,' the petition ran, 'that the Port of Surat is the gate for Mecca from whence many both rich and poor used formerly to go on Moor ships annually to Haj paying passage money or not as their circumstances would admit of but this they are not now permitted to do on Indian ships, therefore the Sheriff and Pasha of Basra and Baghdad are displeased.' The English authorities conciliated the petitioners by authorising the captains to accommodate the genuine pilgrim after a thorough verification of his credentials.

The Cooleys and the Company in Western India

Resistance to the company's system of controls was more effectively vocalised by the northern pirates or Cooley rovers, whose opposition continued well into the first decade of the nineteenth century. The word Cooley seems to have been a generic term including a miscellany of coastal chiefs operating off the littoral of Cutch and Kathiawad. Operating from coastal bases, they attacked ships plying down the coasts, confiscating their cargo and even taking members of the crew as prisoners. Their activities were not exclusively maritime; they maintained important links with the powers in the mainland. The ports of Novabunder, Sootrapara, Porbandar, Dwarka, Verawal and Beyt from where the Cooleys operated were technically under the suzerainty of the Nawab of Junagadh and the Raja of Porbandar who found it to their advantage to aid and abet their operations. According to Robert Holford, the English resident at Cambay in the early years of the nineteenth century, the Cooleys were led by the notorious Syed brothers who employed fast moving gallivats and single decked dinghies.

The activities of the Cooley rovers intensified in the latter decades of the eighteenth and the early years of the nineteenth century when there was a marked expansion of the coastal traffic in cotton in response to the China trade of the Bombay merchants. Attacks on cotton boats caused consternation among Bombay's merchant fraternity who urged the company authorities to take prompt action. In 1799, the Surat Chief and Council raised the issue of countering Cooley piracy. In their notices to Bombay, they pointed out that there were only two ways of dealing with the problem. One was to annex a part of the coast occupied by the rovers and thereby check their depredations as well as undermine the jurisdiction of the mainland rulers in Kathiawad who secretly aided and abetted the operations of the pirates. The other option was to step up defence measures by employing a number of fishing boats like the Versowa armed-boat with strong detachments of sepoys and an armed European in command. The first of the two options required careful consideration: the conquest of the coast had to be judiciously planned given the overarching presence of the Marathas in the coast.

Mr. Cherry, the English Commercial Resident at Surat argued that conquest could not be a permanent solution: 'Even if the Company were in possession of the whole coast from Bombay to the mouth of the Indus, there would still be coolies or pirates to infest the seas which swarm so much with rich and defenceless traders, exclusive of those carrying English passes. The awe in which Cooleys formerly stood of the Company's cruisers is waning off, and it is now become necessity a convoy vessel should be something more than a mere leader or a firer of shots which the Coolies know cannot reach them.' Cherry admitted that the present convoy could not always include the whole of the trade and that boats had to sail without escort. In his view, the existing arrangements were not adequate; 'the system is unequal to the intention, but the defective part now having been ascertained, the remedy is obvious; it is only necessary to apply it by an increase of efficient vessels or proper regulations for granting and taking advantage of the convoys.' The English Chief, Daniel Seton, in his minute dated 20 July 1799 concurred with this suggestion and advised an immediate destruction of Cooley boats before they could be put to sea. This was to be followed up by employing a cruiser of sufficient force with armed vessels to undertake constant patrolling of the coasts to prevent pirate boats from putting out to sea.

These suggestions were endorsed by the whole-hearted support of the Bombay merchants who clamoured for greater protection and convoys to safeguard their cotton investments coming down from Gujarat. Convoy services were stepped up and the coast was vigorously patrolled by the Bombay Marine. By the 1820s, piracy had been effectively curbed and a uniform set of controls enforced along the entire littoral obliging every seafarer to avail of English passes and colours. The merchants engaged in coastal trade benefited from the English convoy and expanded their operations in response to the growing demands of Bombay coastal society, notwithstanding the violence of the encounter between the Bombay Marine and the local potentates, reoriented itself to the new order. Further, the requirements of the Bombay Marine and dockyard in terms of labour recruitment enabled seafaring groups to fit their traditional occupations and skills into the new set up. It was with the advent of steam shipping that the big change came for traditional seafaring groups whose position was even more marginalised.

The operations of the Company's Marines in Bengal and Madras have not received adequate attention from scholars. However, studies on the regional dimensions of the eighteenth century crisis underscore the destruction of the traditional trading structure and displacement of local commercial and seafaring groups. War and dislocation were the distinguishing features of the political situation in the Coromandel in the eighteenth century. This put pressure on local traders who enjoyed little or no protection. Under the circumstances, trade tended to gravitate towards the Indo-British system which had consolidated itself in and around Madras. This new structure, however, as Ashin Dasgupta points out, lacked the quality of freedom which the Mughal system with all its caprices had ensured in the seventeenth century. Men who refused to barter their independence for conditional security and prosperity went under. The Muslim shippers of Masulipatam languished, losing out in the political convulsions that racked the region for the greater part of the century. Admittedly, as recent researches have demonstrated, avenues for survival existed and trading groups such as the Chulias continued to trade extensively with South East Asia. It was thus not entirely fortuitous that when the English settlement was founded in Penang in 1789, the Chulias were among the first settlers to surface. Some years later, when Sir Standford Raffles founded Singapore, the Chulias were found to be its first inhabitants.

The decline of Hugli and the rise of the Calcutta fleet constituted striking developments in the changing trading scenario of Bengal in the course of the first half of the eighteenth century. By 1715, as Peter Marshall's work demonstrates, more ships visited Calcutta than Hugli. In the troubled decades of the 1730s and 1740s, the disparity became even more marked with an increasing numbers of Asian merchants voluntarily switching over to the English shipping. Gujarati traders were among the greatest users of English shipping which enjoyed the reputation of being seaworthy and capable of dealing with piracy on the high seas. The Muslim prominence in the overseas trade was a thing of the past as a substantial portion of the trade with South East Asia was taken over by private traders. N.K. Sinha identified a small number of Muslim merchants doing business on a limited scale—Abdul Rahim, Abdul Ally, Aga Mirza Shirazi, Mirza Mehmud, Aga Ibrahim, Ghulam Hossain—all of whom were sending merchandise to Java, Singapore, Pegu, Mauritius and Suez but mostly in British ships. Independent. Muslim shipping was non-existent by the end of the eighteenth century, a testimony to the overarching hegemony of English private trade and fortunes. In terms of crew, English ships used local sailors and seamen whose livelihood was increasingly tied to the new trading structure developed by the English.

The dismantling of the traditional trading structure was for a medley of indigenous seafaring groups an unmitigated disaster. Not all of them could adapt themselves to the newly emerging trading structure under the aegis of the English East India Company and the restrictive regime it inaugurated. Coastal society underwent a profound change as the English East India Company imposed its unique brand of political authority through the agency of the cartaz and the guns of the marines. The trader and seafarer had to give up much of his autonomy under the new dispensation and was compelled to operate within a set of rigidly defined regulations. These were not always restrictive or crippling; on many occasions, they served to provide material support and immunity against piracy on the high seas. Further, the requirements of the new colonial cities of Calcutta, Bombay and Madras generated employment opportunities for seamen and sailors and other coastal groups like boatmen and fishers. The same could, however, not be said of the traders whose operations did not dovetail with the workings of the newly emerging colonial economy. The new trading structure pushed old commercial groups to the fringes. Of these, some of the more enterprising mercantile communities were able to bounce back and undertake commercial operations in sectors outside the colonial system. Many went under, but not all. New researches have located a range of commercial and financial activities that seafaring communities like the Chulias, Bhatias and Lohanas pursued. Their success stories, however, cannot obscure the divisive and dislocating aspect of the colonial system as it operated on the coasts and the seas.

The Parting of Ways

The segregation of Indian shipping and seafaring from European maritime enterprise under the British Raj constitutes one of the most striking developments of the nineteenth century. Until then, Indian business and seafaring had more or less fitted, even if uneasily, into the framework of the new political system under English dispensation. Banias,

Dubashes and commission agents emerged as subordinate partners of European merchants and agency houses providing them with essential marketing skills and information, wares and even occasionally, capital. Some of them built fortunes around the imperial connection, others were even more enterprising and struck a deal with American businessmen in Calcutta around the first decades of the nineteenth century. One just has to recall the career of Ramdulal Dey who managed the affairs of fifteen Boston houses, fifteen New York houses, one in Philadelphia, one in Salem and two in Newbury port and one in Marblehead. In western India, both Parsi merchants as well as Gujarati and Marwari Bania businessmen successfully operated the trade in raw cotton and opium with China. Even seafaring groups were able to regroup taking advantage of the revival of Arab power under Muscat which stepped up commercial exchanges in the western Indian Ocean. Besides, coastal trade and short haul voyages remained the preserve of indigenous mariners who operated the feeder routes. Coastal trade was by no means insignificant in terms of value or volume and along with internal trade sustained the working of the imperial economic system dominated by the colonial rulers.

Developments in course of the nineteenth century exposed the fragility of the Indo-British partnership that had developed in the preceding century and drew a clearer line of demarcation marking off the white space from the native one. What made this possible was the technological revolution which fundamentally transformed the position of British trade and capital in the Indian subcontinent and the Indian Ocean. The establishment and extension of the railway grid into the Indian heartland, the development of steam ship services, the introduction of telegraphs and the opening of the Suez Canal combined to produce a gigantic, global system of information that could be satisfactorily harnessed to British commercial activities. Superior technology invested the European trading firms with a power that was expressed in all sectors of trade. The new technology overwhelmed maritime Asia; it was not accessible to non-Europeans who could therefore, no longer seriously compete within the new order.

Under the new system, India's foreign trade passed into the hands of European merchants. At the core of the new European shipping monopoly, was the Conference System. This consisted of a series of monopoly rings to exclude all competition by techniques such as rate wars and deferred rebates. Drawing support from government contracts, the Peninsular and Oriental Company and the British Indian Steam Navigation Company came to dominate India's overseas trade and coastal shipping. Native shipping, already in the doldrums, was swept clean from the runs on which the liners came to operate.

The Peninsular and Oriental Company formed the first shipping ring called the Calcutta Conference with a few other steam ship lines of London, Glasgow and Liverpool in 1875 to prevent all comers from entering their preserve. At first applied to the shipment of Manchester goods to India, this system was extended to the China trade in 1879 and by 1899, it came to cover practically all cargo shipped outwards from the United Kingdom except for the Atlantic trade. Over time, the shipping conferences and the managing agency oligopolies became interlocked. The shipping conferences of British steamship companies locally administered in Calcutta by leading European managing agencies monopolised the trade in the Indian Ocean. The conferences that led the way were the British Indian Steam Navigation Company and Messrs Currie's Australian and Indian Line, Messrs Apcar & Company and the Indo China Steam Navigation Company for China steamers sailing to Hong Kong and the straits, British India Steam Navigation Company and Messrs Bullard & King's Natal Line of Steamers and the Bibby Line which confined itself to the Calcutta-England line not touching Rangoon.

These European shipping lines were assisted by leading European exporters organised as managing agencies who functioned as their agents. Together, they enforced a stranglehold over the export business, which the Indian shipper and export merchant could hardly hope to penetrate. Indian enterprise thus turned to the sectors of internal as well as coastal trade and the carrying trade in the western Indian Ocean. Indian merchant capital was able to work out its own sphere of operations and penetrated into East Africa, in the slave and clove trade of Zanzibar, pearl trading in the Gulf and Red Sea among others. Indian commercial and financial groups enjoyed a measure of autonomy and pre-eminence in the western Indian Ocean as financiers, investors and commercial agents.

The resilience of indigenous mercantile activity in the nineteenth century and the relative success of Indian mercantile groups in West Asia and Africa did not alter the fact of dislocation that imperialism engendered in the traditional economies of maritime Asia. All workers of the sea were fundamentally affected by the development of European global hegemony that displaced traders and seafarers. Sailors were reduced to the status of poorly paid labourers and maritime merchants to that of small time traders handling subsidiary businesses. Indian seamen suffered discrimination in terms of wages and provisions in the nineteenth century when they were recruited by Europeans. Employment in European ships was not a new experience for the Indian mariner—as early as the seventeenth century, the English East India Company had been forced to supplement crews decimated by disease and desertion for the return voyage. What was new and different about nineteenth century patterns of recruitment was the systematic discrimination Indian seamen suffered. Bereft of engineering skills which were so essential in an age of steam, Indian sailors were more often than not used in the capacity of deckhands, cooks, stewards and launderers.

The coastal trading sector, too, did not remain entirely unaffected by British steam shipping, the success of which was largely due to the assistance of the British Government and the Government of India. While this restricted the growth of Indian owned steam shipping enterprise, the same could not be said of native craft that remained an important part of coastal traffic. The term native craft referred largely to indigenous Indian Ocean sailing vessels such as dhows, pattamars, baggalas and dhonies. These vessels were an important component of coastal trade and in the latter decades of the nineteenth century accounted for approximately seventy nine percent of all sailing tonnage. Andrew Pope suggests a number of reasons for the continued use of native craft particularly on the west coast. He points out that even though British steam shipping was able to offer services to small merchants trading small amounts of miscellaneous cargo, there were still a greater number of small ports that depended upon the tonnage supplied by sailing vessels. The geographical configurations of the Indian coast prevented steamers from calling at certain ports while many trade routes between small ports were not remunerative for steam ships to enter. Furthermore in some areas like the western littoral, sailing crafts were orientated towards specific trades leaving the larger business of regional trade to other kinds of vessels. For instance, there were the fishing vessels in the Cambay region, whose owners, James Hornell noted, combined fishing with coastal trading due to siltation problems of the estuaries and the limited supply of fish in home waters. The machua boats fished off the south Kathiawad coast in season, and when this was over, switched over to cargo carrying. This switch was made possible thanks to the inherent flexibility in indigenous boat designs, a fact that quite clearly underlines the importance of indigenous technology in sustaining local commercial and seafaring activity in an era of ruthless imperial domination.

Pope's views are in a sense reminiscent of John Edye's description of indigenous sailing craft employed by the inhabitants of the coasts of Coromandel, Malabar and the island of Ceylon. Writing around the turn of the century, he stressed the fact that among all the 'numerous vessels of every class and description which traverse the Ocean, there is a peculiarity of form and construction intended to meet the various localities of the ports or seas in which they are navigated and perhaps in no part of the globe is this principle more fully displayed than in the Indian seas and on the southern peninsula of India including the island of Ceylon where the nature and change of seasons, the monsoons and navigation of the seas and rivers are singularly well provided for, by the truly ingenious and efficient means adopted by the natives in the formation of their rude but most useful vessels.' Referring to the catamarans of Ceylon, Malabar and the Coromandel, he observed that they were particularly well suited to the business of pearl fishing. For fishing, canoes were converted into double platform canoes to transport cattle and other burdensome articles across rivers.

In western India, Edye noticed Pattamars used for coasting trade. There were ghurrabs or grabs as the English called them, equipped with a prow stem which was the same length as the keel with a dead weight capacity of two hundred tons burden. There were in fact several categories of coasting boats operated generally by fishermen of the Mappilla caste in Kerala all of which impressed the writer who even suggested their absorption into the Navy. 'It would be worthy of consideration and a great service to have one of these boats with a native crew attached to each ship for the purpose of saving the seamen and ships and boats from exposure to the intense heat of the sun, the bad effects of which are very sensibly felt by Europeans at all times.' Even if it is argued that the glowing ethnographic notices of indigenous craft and navigation techniques were projected primarily to augment the strength of the English marine force with the use of cheap Indian maritime labour, it also testifies to the resilience and vitality of the indigenous mariner who never stopped experimenting and improving upon his existing pool of resources to drive his traditional occupations of fishing and trading even amidst change and challenge.

NOTES AND REFERENCES

The crisis of the eighteenth century has been more than adequately covered by Ashin Dasgupta in his monograph on Surat, reference to which has been made earlier. The rise of the Calcutta fleet and the changing equations of Indo-British enterprise is brought out in vivid detail by Peter Marshall, *East Indian Fortunes: The British in Bengal in the Eighteenth Century*, (Oxford, 1976). An earlier but useful account of the decline of indigenous enterprise is to be found in N.K. Sinha, *The Economic History of Bengal*. Vol. III, (Calcutta, 1970). For an analysis of Indian mercantile fortunes in the period of transition in the second half of the eighteenth century, see Lakshmi Subramanian, *Indigenous Capital and Imperial Expansion: Bombay, Surat and the West Coast*, (Delhi, 1996). Kenneth McPherson's *The Indian Ocean*, (Delhi, 1993) outlines the principal changes in the trading world of the Indian Ocean following the establishment of the colonial empires of the nineteenth century. 'All indigenous workers and travellers of the Ocean,' he writes, 'were affected by the development of European global hegemony. Indigenous sailors were reduced to labourers on European owned shipping. Indigenous maritime merchants were transformed from rivals and partners of European enterprise to collaborators in the expansion of Western capitalism throughout the Indian Ocean region of the global economy.'

The details on the conference system were worked out on the basis of information provided by Dr. Rajat Kanta Ray, Department of History, Presidency College, Calcutta. For Indian coastal trade and the impact of British steam shipping on it, see Andrew Pope, 'British Steam Shipping and the Indian Coastal Trade 1870-1915', *Indian Economic and Social History Review* Vol. XXXII, No. 1, January-March, 1995. Also see John Edye, 'Description of the Various Classes of Vessels Constructed and Employed by the Natives of the Coasts of Coromandel, Malabar and the Island of Ceylon for Their Coasting Navigation', *Journal of the Royal Asiatic Society of Great Britain and Ireland*. Vol. I, London, 1834.

Seas and Sahebs in Indian Perception: An Epilogue

The establishment of English political power in the Indian sub-continent was integrally related to their maritime dominance which they exercised in no uncertain terms as early as the middle decades of the eighteenth century. On both seaboards of the Indian sub-continent, claims to maritime hegemony were articulated and justified as essential pre-conditions to fair trade and enterprise. These claims were duly enforced as the English East India Company's marine forces cleaned up the trading lanes of the Indian Ocean, established the use of the company's pass as the only admissible trading permit in the high seas and eliminated all resistance from local coastal groups who were dismissed as pirates and chastised accordingly. The English system of naval and maritime controls, even if the most systematised, was neither new nor unprecedented in the annals of maritime India. The Portuguese, the Dutch and even the French and the Danes had instituted a system of passes and permits over the Indian seafarer, a measure that had necessarily involved a certain degree of violence in the interaction between the Europeans and the sea people of India. It is hardly a matter of surprise, therefore, that accounts of the

Indo-European encounter on both sides have been charged with an obvious bias against the other. European travel accounts and official reports invariably constructed lurid images of Indian coastal potentates, reckless in their dealings and oppressive in their conduct towards the fair trader, Indian and European alike. For James Douglas, even a ruler of Shivaji's calibre was in his naval dealings a Maratha pirate more than anything else; there was nothing to commend in his naval policies which were but an expression of naked self-aggrandisement. Indian chroniclers, on their part, had a different story to recount of oppressive Europeans who used their naval strength and stratagem to impose a reign of terror on the high seas. They emphasised the innate cruelty and oppression of the Europeans identified by their top hats and overbearing manner and utter insensitivity to local convention and etiquette. In Malabar for instance, the *Kerala Nama* lamented the fate that had befallen the local inhabitants in the wake of the Portuguese encounter while in Bengal, the Firangis and Harmads became figures of fear and dread. The local ballads which we have had occasion to refer to earlier, transmitted a collective impression of the Portuguese as marauders and slave traders, an impression that never quite faded from local memory and was in fact continually reinforced by popular literature and folklore. The atrocities of the Portuguese, their unwarranted assaults on the high seas and their abominable practices of enslaving women and trafficking in slaves are recurrent motifs that run though the eastern Bengal ballads.

Mughal and late Mughal chroniclers did not differ very much in their representation of the Portuguese and their politics. Even a sensitive writer like Mirza Ihtisamuddin referred to the needless aggression of the Portuguese, an impression that had obviously been transmitted through popular perception as well as historical writings like those of Khafi Khan. In fact, the image of the Portuguese as the unlawful and rapacious aggressor was a persistent one that was re-invoked in modern fiction, even more than the travails of the colonial encounter which by its nature, complexity and trajectory met with a different and more ambivalent reception. It may well be argued that the representation of the Portuguese as aggressors who brought sorrow to the sacred realm was very much in the nature of a nationalist outrage against Western enslavement of all kinds. The experience of colonial rule with strong racial overtones under the British, however, brought in further accretions to existing perceptions of the seas and the European factor, the two in a sense being intertwined. Historians, litterateurs and travellers attempted in their own ways to explore the myriad dimensions of the Indo-European encounter that had been from the very outset mediated through the seas. This chapter proposes to examine some of these accounts as a means of situating the sea, seafarers and Europeans in Indian perception and representation. The texts chosen for this purpose are the *Vilayat Nama* (1765) by Mirza Ihtisamuddin, the travel diaries of Rabindranath Tagore, *Europe Jatrir Diary* (4 August November, 1890) and the novel *Rakta Sandhya* (1930) by Saradindu Bandopadhyaya. Of these, two are in Bengal which in itself says something of the proximity of the European experience to Bengal. The *Vilayat Nama*, on the other hand, is a historical account of Mirza Ihtisamuddin's travels to England and of his experiences abroad and one of the earliest accounts to highlight the East-West encounter from the Indian perspective. It is an account that is sweeping in its range and accurate in detail but is refreshingly free from prejudice and the paranoia that colonialism engendered in its subjects.

Mirza Ihtisamuddin wrote the *Vilayat Nama* in 1765. His connection with the English East India Company was a close one. Not only did he function as Carnac's munshi, he was also instrumental in drafting the *Diwani Sanad* transferring to the company the right to the surplus revenues of Bengal, Bihar and Orissa. He was the first Indian to visit England and embarked on the Courville for his outward journey. His initial enthusiasm was tinged with anxiety as he spoke of undergoing the 'most frightful pangs of separation from his homeland that only the Almighty could comprehend'. That did not deter him from appreciating the spirit of European enterprise that had successfully charted unknown seas. His description of the sea of Oman was thus prefaced by a catalogue of the multiple endeavours of the Europeans to fathom the depths of the ocean, a description of the compass and of the contrasting terms of reference used by navigators. Thus while the Muslims calculated their direction from the west, the hat wearing foreigners used the north as their principal reference point. Mirza was particularly observant when it came to describing ships, masts and sails. He identifies a single-mast ship as the sloop, a two-masted one as the ghurrab (later known and distorted as Grab) and a three-masted one as the ship. A ship usually had five decks, the topmost deck belonged to the captain and his select colleagues and where valuables were stored. On the second deck, at the rear, space was hired out to travellers in the form of small cabins. There was a kitchen in the front while the space between the kitchen and cabins was occupied by the khalasis or sailors who slept in hammocks strung from the roof. The middle deck had two cannons stationed on either side. Food and other provisions were stored on the third deck while the items of trade were carefully spaced in the fourth deck leaving the fifth free for ballast.

Like his European counterparts, Ihtisamuddin demonstrated great curiosity about winds and wind systems. He had clearly no access to scientific information but the deficiency was more than made up by his pragmatic understanding of adverse and favourable winds and the seaworthy nature of the East Indian men. It was without the slightest rancour that he mentioned an incident when the ship in which he was aboard was being tossed about by gusty winds. Apprehending the worst, he expressed his anxieties to the captain, Mr. Swinton, who also happened to be a personal friend. Swinton made light of the matter, and as Ihtisamuddin writes, jocularly dismissed his anxieties by quipping that 'this is not your country's vessel that it should sink'. Ihtisamuddin admitted that Europeans were superior in the art of navigation and made constant efforts to upgrade their skills and were also able to withstand great physical strain. This was strikingly displayed whenever sails had to be furled and unfurled and masts had to be repaired during storms. He also admired the proficiency and curiosity of the Europeans in scientific matters, a fact that struck him even more forcefully in England where he had the opportunity of surveying their educational system.

In London, the author was something of a novelty attracting the curiosity of local men and women. Ihtisamuddin was warm in his praise of lovely English ladies and their courteous disposition and seems to have been quite flabbergasted as they swarmed around him asking in jest 'my dear, kiss me'. He attributed his popularity and appeal to his apparel; it was summer time and he was dressed in a long dress, pajamas, a handkerchief wound around his neck, embroidered slippers and a cummerbund. He was struck by the popularity of music and dance which was appreciated by a wide segment of the population cutting across divisions of class and status. Everyone from the nobleman to the commoner flocked in to see dance and musical performances. This, according to Mirza, was in sharp contrast to the scene in India, where music and dance and indeed the entire gamut of performing arts remained tied to court patronage which gave the nobility privileged access to the same. In fact, the English social system, their education, not to speak of their military skill, were far superior to anything that India had to offer. The English spared no efforts in constantly improving their lot; idleness and indolence was antithetical to their nature. Ihtisamuddin was particularly impressed by the emphasis that was placed on education and admired the rigour that characterised the efforts of English parents in bringing up and educating their wards. Indian parents by contrast were blind in their affection for their offspring and even went to the extent of depriving them of education and discipline. In effect, they damned their wards to a life of permanent deprivation, drudgery and darkness.

Ihtisamuddin was, however, no anglophile. He engaged in lively debates with his English patrons and upheld the moral superiority of Islam and its value system. On one occasion, he actually defended the Islamic custom of taking four wives and asked the members whether they could actually swear that they knew of any man with a monogamous relationship who had never coveted another woman or another man's wife. Silence greeted this awkward and unexpected salvo and Ihtisamuddin felt that he had, in fact scored a point or two. Also, he genuinely believed that it was better to be poor in his own country rather than being rich in England, and that Indian women were more endearing than their white counterparts. What in fact comes through clearly in Ihtisamuddin's account is his attachment to Hindustan which was grounded in both emotional reality as well as in his social context. Explaining why he would not consider taking an English wife, he said that it would be difficult for him to do so on account of two reasons. As an aristocrat in his country, Ihtisamuddin could not contemplate a match with a person who came from a lower status group. On the other hand, an arrangement with a social equal was out of the question, for the lady whom he would favour would not reciprocate his feelings because he 'would be beneath her station'.

Ihtisamuddin's attachment to Hindustan, the land of his birth and of his choice and his sadness at the passing away of the Mughal order did not cloud his perception of the English, his appreciation of their social system and moral order which he admitted to being superior. This was indeed a far cry from the nationalist construction of the European legacy both in fiction as well as in non fictional narratives. For Ihtisamuddin, the traversing of the seas and the *Vilayat* was an enriching experience that brought him closer to understanding the powerful European who had successfully charted the seas and subjugated the Mughal to make Hindustan his fief. As a member of the gentry whose political existence was dependent on English patronage, it is understandable why Ihtisamuddin did not dwell on the dislocation that accompanied the advent of the Europeans at land and sea.

The representation of colonial dominion and the complexity of its psychological impact stands in marked contrast to early representations of the Portuguese whose presence in coastal society had been conspicuous. The Portuguese were almost always identified with piracy and brigandage. With the colonial experience, the transmission of images was different, more nuanced and ambivalent. This is best illustrated in Rabindranath Tagore's writings. European civilisation evoked a curious medley of responses from Tagore; he was aware of its strength and potent attraction but could not help associating it with domination and power that had enslaved Indians for so long. 'How I wish,' he wrote 'I could embrace my India and shield her from all the insults heaped on her. The Sahibs kick us all the time, yet we do not leave their doorstop. Where they do not let us enter with our shoes on, we leave our shoes behind. Where they do not allow us to enter with our heads held high, we enter with bowed heads. Where we are denied admittance as Indians, we go in the guise of Englishmen. They do not want us and yet we find excuses, we cringe and cower and at the slightest opportunity we try and seek their company isolating ourselves from our countrymen and even joining them in the abuse of the nation.' On the same occasion, he asked himself why India had had to absorb the pain of European domination which was psychologically so debilitating. 'Why did we have to be taken by this raging flood of humanity. Here, we were secure in our refuge, our minds closed and the world shut out. Where was the tiny crack that let in the raging flood which swept us off our feet and confused us so?'

The pain of subjugation and the deeper sense of emotional attachment to the nation lent a different aspect to Tagore's handling of the East-West encounter. In marked contrast to Ihtisamuddin, who felt no malice about the gushing English ladies who flocked around him begging to be kissed, Tagore was critical of English women in society. 'What do they do the rest of the time? They generally subscribe to Mudle's Library whence they borrow novels which they devour increasingly. Besides this, there is of course the business of flirting. What is flirting? It is to feign love. Both sides know there is no genuine emotion involved, nonetheless they giggle and mouth pleasant nothings. Occasionally, the lady happens to act coy and sulk, at which the partner, taking cue, tries to assuage her. If he happens to say something mildly amusing the lady retorts, Oh you naughty, wicked, provoking man. This interchange of verbal repartee and display of affection is what is known as flirting in the sense that it indicates a relationship of greater depth and permanence. However, it is difficult to comment on how permanent these encounters are. But then it is almost a fad to sigh, swoon and to blush. Indeed the devouring of romantic novelettes is largely responsible for this state. Thus receiving friends, social visits, reading more novels, creating new fashions, emulating them, flirting and falling in love all these occupy much of their time.' And yet Tagore was on more than one occasion impressed with the level of awareness and education that middle class ladies possessed. They were not confined to their houses, they socialised and interacted freely, they were ready to air their views in a gathering and participate meaningfully in a conversation. These sentiments in a sense were not necessarily contradictory; they expressed only too well the complexity of the colonial impact on its subjects, an impact that did not lend itself easily to either a complete rejection of the colonial presence or to a slavish limitation of its architects. With the Portuguese, the representation was much easier. Here was a chapter in the annals of the country's medieval past which underscored all too clearly the conflict between the crude and barbarous Portuguese pirate and the suave, law abiding Asian trader who plied his trade in a gentle and well ordered world that had not known the use of arms or force. The marginality of the Portuguese presence made it easier to deal with them, and their brutality was recast within a romantic mould to valourise the nation's historic past.

The novel *Rakta Sandhya* (A Bloody Sunset) by Saradindu Bandopadhyay is set in the historic city of Calicut, famed for its wares, for its cosmopolitanism and the benevolence of its rulers who welcomed to this city traders from far and wide of every conceivable extraction. The city stood at the cross roads of the Indian Ocean. Chinese, Moors and Bengalis frequented its roadsteads and some even took up permanent residence like the story's protagonist Mirza Daud bin Ghulam Siddiqi, a Moor from Morocco. The world they inhabited was a gentle one—there were profits for everyone to be made in fair and proper business transactions, there was justice to be had at the court of the Zamorin, the ruler, and there were good times to look forward to, particularly for Daud as he had recently been blessed with a baby daughter.

The situation however dramatically changed with the coming of the Portuguese and their strong arm tactics which filled the trading world of Hind with a sense of grim apprehension and helplessness. Daud was the butt of Portuguese aggression; as a Moor who signalled his protest against the new comers, he was singled out for punishment, which finally came on the high seas. Returning from the Haj, with his aged father, young wife and baby daughter, Daud had the misfortune of falling prey to the marauding armada that scoured the Red Sea waiting for Asian ships to fall within the Portuguese dragnet. The story ended with Daud's vain resistance and the tragic deaths of his family members at the hands of the avenging Vasco da Gama, who had been slighted three years ago in Calicut by Daud who had seen through the motives of Gama and his associates. In fact, the latter had made no attempt to conceal their hatred and contempt for the Moors whom they wished to eliminate from the trading channels of the Indian Ocean.

In terms of execution, the novel is not merely evocative but also rather accurate in identifying the military dimension of the Portuguese entry into the trading world of the Indian Ocean. The reader is transported to a trading world that lived by a different set of conventions that the Portuguese not only failed to understand but which they wilfully flouted. Thus we have references to the Portuguese offering unusually high prices for items of trade in order to ingratiate themselves with the city's merchants and thereby neutralise the opposition of the Moors. The deployment of brute force to control trade is symbolised by the final, bloody encounter between Daud and Gama—the blood and the gore reflected in the brilliant crimson hues of sunset that remained a mute witness to the tragedy.

What is striking about the novel is the manner in which the Portuguese entry into the trading world of India has been portrayed. The novelist clearly drew from a long tradition, both written and oral, which had emphasised the violence of the encounter with the Harmads. Chroniclers like Khaf Khan along with the bards and boatmen of eastern Bengal had continually invoked the bloody image of the Portuguese, the dreaded Harmads and Firangis who terrorised the seafarer, ran a vile traffic in slaves and abducted women. It was thus possible for a modern novelist like Saradindu to situate the encounter in more complex terms, in a material context that was historically more accurate and in consonance with popular perception. The persistence of the imagery of the Portuguese as the apostles of piracy and violence remained, in the final analysis, a reflection of the vitality of popular perception and received traditions.

Appendices

The extracts that make up the following appendices have been selected to highlight some of the major themes that stand out in our understanding of the material context in which Indian seafaring operated over time. The continental preoccupation of the ruling authorities, like the Mughal State for example, forced indigenous seafarers and traders to develop their own strategies of survival and success. The establishment of the imperial admiralty by the Mughals with much fanfare did not reflect a conscious maritime interest on the part of the State; rather it was designed to supplement military operations on land and safeguard, to a measure, riverine traffic (See Appendix 1).

European aggression at sea was an important determinant of coastal society. While researches have indubitably established the fact that the activities and aggression of the Portuguese in the sixteenth century and of their North European successors thereafter, failed to depress or even divert Indian trading operations in the Indian Ocean, it is also important to stress the psychological impact of the European encounter on coastal society. Folk traditions in coastal Bengal conveyed the impression of violence that the Portuguese brought in their wake. The eastern Bengal ballads deserve mention in this connection. An extract from the ballad of Nasar Malum

(See Appendix II) will serve to illustrate the impact that the Harmads had on the inhabitants of coastal Bengal.

Finally, there is an extract from Major Walker's correspondence in Baroda in the early nineteenth century (See Appendix III) to underscore the participation of Hindu commercial groups in overseas trade. Major Walker commented on the presence of Bania colonies in West Asia—a point that suggests the social acceptability of sea travel among high caste Hindu groups.

Appendix-I—Description of the Mughal Admiralty in the *Ain i Akbari* Vol I, by Abul Fazl Allami. Translated into English by H. Blochmann, edited by D.C. Phillott, Reprint, Crown Publications, New Delhi, 1988. pp. 289-292.

The Admiralty

This department is of great use for the successful operations of the army, and for the benefit of the country in general; it furnishes means of obtaining things of value, provides for agriculture, and His Majesty's household. His Majesty, in fostering this source of power, keeps four objects in view, and looks upon promoting the efficiency of this department as an act of divine worship.

First—The fitting out of strong boats, capable of carrying elephants. Some are made in such a manner as to be of use in sieges and for the conquest of strong forts. Experienced officers look upon ships as if they were houses and dromedaries and use them as excellent means of conquest. So especially in Turkey, Zanzibar, and Europe. In every part of His Majesty's empire ships are numerous; but in Bengal, Kashmir, and Thathah (Sind) they are the pivot of all commerce. His Majesty had the sterns of the boats made in shape of wonderful animals, and thus combines terror with amusement. Turrets and pleasing kiosks, markets, and beautiful flower-beds, have likewise been constructed on the rivers. Along the coasts of the ocean, in the west, east, and south of India, large ships are built, which are suitable for voyages. The harbours have been put into excellent condition, and the experience of seamen has much improved. Large ships are also built at Ilahabad and Lahor, and are then sent to the coast. In Kashmir, a model of a ship was made which was much admired.

Secondly—To appoint experienced seamen acquainted with the tides, the depths of the ocean, the time when the several winds blow, and their advantages and disadvantages. They must be familiar with shallows and banks. Besides, a seaman must be hale and strong, a good swimmer, kind hearted, hard working, capable of bearing fatigue, patient; in fact, he must possess all good qualities. Men of such character can only be found after much trouble. The best seamen come from Malibar (Malabar).

Boatmen also bring men and their things from one side of the river to the other.

The number of sailors in a ship varies according to the size of the vessel. In large ships there are twelve classes. 1. The *Nakhuda*, or owner of the ship. This word is evidently a short form of *Navkhuda*. He fixes the course of the ship. 2. The *Muallim*, or Captain. He must be acquainted with the depths and the shallow places of the ocean, and must know astronomy. It is he who guides the ship to her destination, and prevents her from falling into dangers. 3. The *Tamdil*[1] or chief of the *khalasis*, or sailors. Sailors, in seamen's language, are called *khalasis* or *kharwas*. 4. The *Nakhuda-khashab*. He supplies the passengers with firewood and straw, and assists in shipping and unlading the cargo. 5. The *Sarhang*, or mate, superintends the docking and

[1]Tandail or tandel, H.—P.

landing of the ship and often acts for the *Muallim*. 6. The *Bhandari* has the charge of the stores. 7. The *Karrani*[2] is a writer who keeps the accounts of the ship, and serves out water to the passengers. 8. The *Sukkangir*,[3] or helmsman. He steers the ship according to the orders of the *Muallim*. Some ships carry several helmsmen, but never more than twenty. 9. The *Panjari* looks out from the top of the mast, and gives notice when he sees land or a ship, or a coming storm, etc. 10. The *Gumti* belongs to the class of *khalasis*. He throws out the water which has leaked through the ship. 11. The *Top-andaz*, or gunner, is required in naval fights; the number depends on the size of the ship. 12. The *Kharwa* or common sailors. They set and furl the sails. Some of them perform the duty of divers, and stop leaks, or set free the anchor when it sticks fast. The amount of their wages varies, and depends on the voyage, or *kush*, as seamen call it. In the harbour of *Satgaw* (*Hugli*) a *Nakhuda* gets 400 R.; besides, he is allowed four *malikh*, or cabins, which he fills with wares for his own profit. Every ship is divided into several divisions, for the accommodation of passengers and the storage of goods, each of the divisions being called a *malikh*. The *Muallim* gets 200 *R*. and two *malikhs*; the *Tandil*, 120 *R*.; the *Karrani*, 50 R.; and one *malikh*; the *Nakhuda khashab*, 30 *R*.; the *Sarhang*, 25 *R*.; the *Sukkangir*, *Panjari*, and *Bhandari*, each 15 *R*.; each *Kharwa* or common sailor, 40 R., and his daily food in addition; the *Degandaz*, or *gunner*, 12 *R*.

In *Kambhayat* (Cambay), a *Nakhuda* gets 800 *R*., and the other men in the same proportion. In *Lahari*, a *Nakhuda* gets 300 R., and the rest in proportion.

---

[2]This word is nowadays pronounced *Kirani*, and is applied to any clerk. The word is often used contemptuously.

[3]There is a modern Anglo-Indian word used in Calcutta, 'sea-cunny', derived from *sukkani*.—P.

In *Achin*, he gets half as much again as in southern harbours; in Portugal, two and a half as much again; and in Malacca,[1] twice as much again. In Pegu and Dahnasari, he gets half as much again as in Cambay. All these rates vary according to the place and the length of the voyage. But it would take me too long to give more details.

Boatmen on rivers have wages varying from 100 to 500 d. *per mensem*.

Thirdly—an experienced man has been appointed to look after the rivers. He must be an imposing and fearless man, must have a loud voice, must be capable of bearing fatigue, active, zealous, kind, fond of travelling, a good swimmer. As he possesses experience, he settles every difficulty which arises regarding fords, and takes care that such places are not overcrowded, or too narrow, or very uneven or full of mud. He regulates the number of passengers which a ferry may carry; he must not allow travellers to be delayed, and sees that poor people are passed over *gratis*. He ought not to allow people to swim across, or wares to be deposited anywhere else but at fording places. He should also prevent people from crossing at night, unless in cases of necessity.

Fourthly—the remission of duties. His Majesty, in his mercy, has remitted many tolls, though the income derived from them equalled the revenue of a whole country. He only wishes that boatmen should get their wages. The state takes certain taxes in harbour places; but they never exceed two and a half per cent., which is so little compared with the taxes formerly levied, that merchants look upon harbour taxes as totally remitted.

The following sums are levied as river tolls. For every boat, 1 *R*. *Per kos* at the rate of 1,000 *mans*, provided the boat and the men belong to one and the same owner. But if the boat belongs to another man and everything in the boat to the man who has hired it, the tax is 1 R. for every 2½ *kos*. At ferry places, an elephant has to pay 10 *d*. for crossing; a laden cart, 4 *d.*; do. Empty, 2 *d.*; a laden camel, 1 *d.*; empty camels, horses, cattle with their things, 1/2 *d.*; do. empty, 1/4 *d.* Other beasts of burden pay 1/16 *d.*, which includes the toll due by the river. Twenty people pay 1 *d.* for crossing; but they are often taken *gratis.*

The rule is that one-half or one-third of the tolls thus collected go to the state (the other half goes to the boatmen).

Merchants are therefore well treated, and the articles of foreign countries are imported in large quantities.

Appendix-II—Extracts from *Nuranneha and the Grave, Eastern Bengal Ballads*, Ramtanu Lahiri Research Fellowships for 1929-31 in two parts. Vol. IV Part I. Compiled and edited by Dineschandra Sen. Published by the University of Calcutta, 1932.

The Harmads (8)

On the west of Rangadia was the illimitable sea. The small island which was brought under the plough quite recently, was gradually increasing in size. Down the sea, when the flow-tide came, the breakers roared and dashed against one another. Many were the Godhu and Balam boats, loaded with rice, which marched through the Bay—their name was legion. The dreaded Portuguese pirates, the Harmads, were constantly watching the movements of these boats, stealthily following them through the nooks of the coast. They plundered the boats and assassinated their crew, and the boatmen and captains of the sea-side trembled in fear of the Harmads.

There is a spot not far from the coast called the Panch Garia[4] (the Five Waves) beyond which is the terrible Bay—

[4]It is a channel lying between Cox's Bazar and Mahishkhali.

the *Kalapani* (*lit.* Black Waters). The waves there are high as mountain-summits and they fiercely played with the wind. The boats and ships were raised to a great height to be thrown down to the lowest pit alternately. When rough gales blew there, all of a sudden the waves of the Panch Garia roared and touched the very heaven in their fierce dance. These waves of the Black Waters are dreadful. Ships with sails puffed up by winds, struggled hard to preserve themselves, and the crew were dismayed when crossing this portion of the deep; and some pledged a thousand rupees to be offered to the great saints if they could go back to the land with safety. The Hindus prayed to Kali and the Mughs (the Burmese) offered prayers to *Phara*, and all cried, 'Oh Lord, save us from this crisis.'

When the fierce *Kalapani* has been crossed, the sea becomes a pleasant sight; it is calm and the new islands look beautiful in the East. These islets have no trees or plants but yet they look fresh and delightful.

But now let us resume the story of the Harmads.

In the upstream of the Bay, there are many turns by the side of the coast; the pirates conceal themselves in these nooks watching the boats. The boats come from foreign countries, earning large profits by trade—their flags are raised high fluttering in the wind. Swift are the small boats of the pirates which pass over the Bay like birds over the sky. The Harmads do not at all care for their lives; they are a set of desperate people and in naval fights they show unflinching courage and tact.

They used to plunder the goods and sink the boats in the depth of the sea. They would sometimes take the boatmen of the ships they plundered captives—bound in chains.

Now, at the time of which we are speaking, Nur and Malek had fallen head-long in love and were enjoying themselves when the Harmads visited the island of Rangadia.

They attacked the house of Azgar, opened the big chest and seized all its contents. Nothing of value was left in the house. Azgar cried like a helpless child and Nur struck her head with her hands. But the tragedy did not end there. The pirates bound both Nur and Malek with ropes and carried them away.

Did they mean to celebrate the marriage of the betrothed pair?

The old peasant, quite helpless, began to cry and his wife joined in his laments. The greatest grief they felt was for their daughter. How tenderly had they cherished the hope of seeing her happy in marriage. (Ll. 1-50.)

Encounter (9)

Playful are these boats of the pirates, They marched, keeping time as it were, with the motion of the waves! Like the vultures that hovered over the sea, they marched flapping their wings of sail. In one of these, lay poor Nur fastened to a cabin. There was no cloth on her person, how could she preserve her decency? The wind had a share in the oppression of the poor girl, for it opened the rich treasure of her hair which fluttered dishevelled on all sides.

The hands of Malek were bound behind his back so tightly that the pain was excruciating and unbearable.

The leader of the gang was charmed with the beauty of Nur. He approached Malek and said, 'What is this girl to you? Who is her father, and who her father-in-law?'

Malek stared at the face of the leader but gave no answer. At this the leader took a sharp dagger in his hand, Nur gave a shrill cry, when all of a sudden a violent gale blew, tearing the ropes of the sails to pieces. Losing the sail the boat fell into one of the dreaded whirlpools which made it reel round and round, till it was carried desperately into a sandy shoal. The red orb was sinking in the western horizon.

There was no plant, no tree in that land far or near;—sand on all sides, and nothing else. A few fishermen were catching fish in the Bay. The whole gang of robbers forcibly entered the boat of these fishermen. Some of them had just kindled fire in the hearth for boiling rice and other were dressing fish, when this great mishap befell them. (Ll. 1-24.)

Retaliation (10)

All the fishermen of the locality in the meantime had gathered there. Some of them were armed with swords, some with ropes of sail and long bamboo poles. Some carried oars and helms and they attacked the robbers in a body. A great skirmish took place in that sandy shore. Many were killed outright and many had their skulls broken.

There was one aged fisherman who came up at this stage with a large quantity of powdered pepper. He threw handfuls of these into the eyes of the robbers. They staggered at this unexpected blow and could not keep standing. They fell down upon the sand. The robbers were disarmed by the fishermen and were bound, hand and foot. Liberally were they served with blows, slaps and kicks.

Having thus made the Harmads captives, the fishermen proceeded to judge the criminals. Some of them set up a great uproar, demanding the indiscriminate massacre of these wicked men; they cried, 'With our sharp daggers let us at once cut off their heads;' but the more merciful ones said, 'No brethren, tie heavy stones with their necks and throw them into the middle of the illimitable sea in that condition.'

When the fishermen were clamourously talking in this manner, Malek overheard their angry speeches,—bound as he was in the dock of the boat of the robbers. Then Malek cried aloud rending the very sky with his lamentations. Some fishermen heard his voice and with torches in their hands came up for enquiry. They took pity on Malek and set him free and heard every thing from his lips from the beginning to the end. Next they went to rescue poor Nur, who had fainted. They raised her up, but her head could not be kept erect. As often as they tried to raise it, it bent down. Malek had her eyes gently opened, but they seemed to be bereft of sight and did not twinkle. There was no sound in her heart, and her pulse did not beat. Her hands and feet had grown cool as ice—she lay thoroughly prostrate and her teeth were clenched.

They brought her to the boat of the fishermen. Some of them poured water on her head and some fanned her; and disconsolate Malek cried all the while like a child at her pitiable condition and lamented wildly. 'Look at me, dear sister, get up and let us once more go to our house at Rangadia,—rise up, oh my full-moon, diffusing light and life! Alas, who will now prepare betels for me? Who will offer me tobacco? In the dry season, who will refresh me by offering cool drink? Rise up, oh lamp of my house! Who will spread a nice mat on the floor for my repose! Rise up dear one, let us go back and you will once more prepare sweet curd for me and store it in new earthen vessels. Then at night we will watch the fowls hatching their eggs in the hut. Wake up from this sleep and let us go back quickly to our deserted home.'

Thus did Malek cry, sitting near the girl, and did not find consolation any way. The old fisherman brought from a little box a pill which he mixed with cool water and made the girl take it. He also sprinkled water all over her face and eyes.

Malek raised her up and placed her in his lap and began to fan her. He said that he perceived a little breath in her nostrils. There, the beams of the moon fell on her beautiful face and the southern wind brought a freshness as it blew over her. A little after the girl opened her eyes.

She sat on her bed and said a word or two. They gave her a handful of rice to eat after having washed it with water. She enquired about her father and mother. Slowly, after a time, did Malek acquaint her with all that had happened.

One of the robbers, kept bound under the deck, had, in the meantime, broken his chain and helped others to do the same. They then silently made their escape, unnoticed by the careless fishermen (Ll. 1-58.)

Extract from *The Ballad of Nasar Malum, Eastern Bengal Ballads*. Pp. 107—150.

(14)

The western sea in those days was the resort of Harmads who plundered all boats and ships that fell in their way. They would loot all they found and if the crew offered anything like resistance, they cut their throats and killed them without mercy. In the immense deep the Harmads were a terror. So the sloops in those days went in a body,—a good number of them together all compact, when they had to travel a long distance by sea. The sailors and the crew took with them guns and gunpowder, spears and other weapons. On the south of the Kaicha lay the port of Diang and from that port the ships all started on sea-voyage, forming a strong fleet ready to meet the foe when occasion arose.

Nasar's sloop came to Gobadhya and was stranded on the sand. This was a notorious resort of the Harmads. Many a sailor and owner of ships had here encountered great dangers. The storm ceased and ebb-tide commenced. The water subsided and the night looked grim in its impenetrable darkness.

The island of Gobadhya was a dreary tract, full of sand and nothing else. Not a grass, not a straw was to be seen there. There was no mark or sign to indicate the way to the traveller, and Nasar could not know his whereabouts nor the direction he should follow. The sand filled the deck of the ship and she became fixed to a spot without any power to move.

In the morning the flow-tide would begin, releasing the ship from her stranded condition. In expectation they all sat together wishing for the approach of the dawn. They guarded with care the wealth that lay in the ship and discussed the way they should take to cross the sea.

The night was nearly over and the first streaks of the east appeared in the horizon. The Harmads were lying in ambush in the western shoals. The sun's disk rose as it were from the sea and peered through the east. At the sight the birds of the sea began to cry wildly, and gradually the flow-tide set in merging the island in water. The Harmads were seen at a distance busy observing their ship with the help of telescopes. Nasar felt a shudder at the sight of the miscreants.

Ten or twelve of them approached Nasar, dressed in black trousers. Some wore short red coats and turbans on their heads. In the belt of their waists they had scabbards bound tightly and they had guns in their hands. The blood flowing in the veins of Nasar became frozen in fear. The captain and the sailors found their limbs paralysed and could not move their hands and feet.

The first thing the robbers did was to hold Nasar tightly by the neck. They slapped his cheeks and the blows were so sudden and severe that Nasar fell down on the deck. His sailors and other men lay more like dead than living beings viewing with their timid eyes the action of the robbers.

The next thing the Harmads did was to bind them all by strong ropes and then enter the ship for plunder.

They discovered great riches by breaking open the chests. Right glad were they to find a large quantity of Burmese gold there. The flow in the sea attained its highest point and it was now an easy task for the robbers to drag down the ship from the sands and float her in the sea. The heaps of dried *Laukha* fish had become wet and now being exposed to the rays of the sun a bad odour emanated from them and hundreds of sea-birds came swooping down from the sky and seized large numbers of these goods. The vultures which flew above the sea, the sea-pigeon and other birds all assembled in huge numbers over this booty, and it became a problem to the robbers as to how to preserve the fish from the birds.

The great ship of Nasar with all its valuable goods was now in the possession of the Harmads and they swiftly marched home-wards with their loot. (Ll. 1-54.)

Appendix-III **The proper term is Wanee or Vanee, or Waneeya, from the Sanskrit Waneek. This word means both a settled and an itinerant Trader. It is therefore applied to any Caste following this Profession, and is not properly speaking a distinction of caste.**

The ancient connexion of Persia, and specially of Arabia with India, may be perceived in the commerce which is carried on at this day between these countries. The Commerce of Arabia and the Western ports of India is very extensive, and there is every reason to conclude that it has existed from the remotest times. The Portuguese found the Arabs settled in Malabar and long before that period they appeared as Soldiers and Merchants in many other parts of India.

At present they Trade not only with India but with the Eastern Islands. As much of this Trade is carried on in small Vessels, it is the less noticed by Europeans, but it is nevertheless of a very great extent. The Trade which they have with Gujarat, Kattywar, Boje and Scind, is considerable. The Banias are their agents, Factors and Brokers, and exercise probably the same Profession which they did in the time of Alexander. At that time they were most likely settled in Arabia and Persia.

The covetous disposition of the Wanee is proverbial. He is restless for gain, and will go any length to acquire it. Although timid and full of prejudice, this insatiable desire induces him to visit foreign Countries. They have established little Colonies in Malaya, and have settled in Persia, Bassorah, the Arabian Gulf and even on the Banks of the Caspian Sea. The Wanee deals in every specie of merchandise, but particularly in Grain. He traffics also largely in cloths, and professes Brokerage, and practices Usury in every shape.

Source: Walker of Bowland Papers 1780—1830 (Acc. 2228) National Library of Scotland, Edinburgh. Letters, Reports & Papers. Histories, An Account of Castes and Professions in Gujarat.